FOR ALL ELECTRONIC KEYBOARDS

easy ELECTRONIC KEYBOARD MUSIC®

THE BIG & EASY SONGBOOK
44

CONTENTS

ISBN 0-7935-0911-4

HAL•LE CORPO

7777 W. BLUEMOUND RD. P.O. BOX 1

D1007449

E-Z PLAY ® TODAY Music Notation © 19
Copyright © 1991 by HAL LEO.
International Copyright Secured   All Rights Reserved

THE BIG & EASY SONGBOOK

ALOHA OE

Regi-Sound Program: 7
Rhythm: Swing or Hawaiian

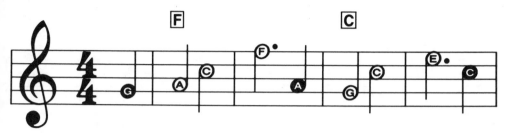

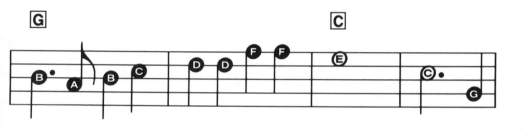

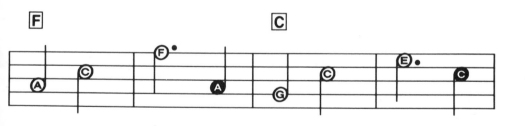

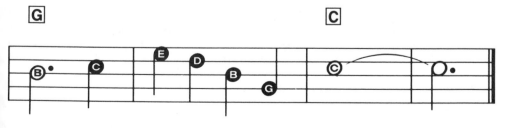

AURA LEE

Regi-Sound Program: 9
Rhythm: Swing

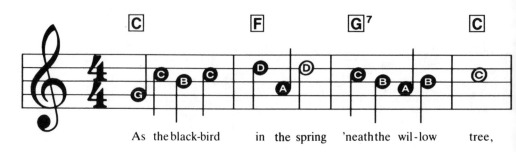

As the black-bird   in the spring   'neath the wil-low   tree,

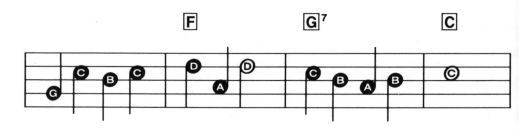

sat and peeped, I   heard him sing,   sing of Au - ra   Lee.

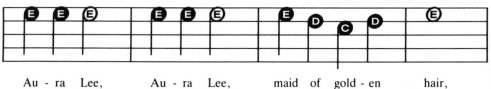

Au - ra Lee,   Au - ra Lee,   maid of gold - en   hair,

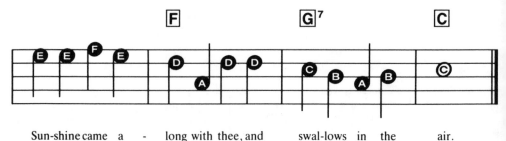

Sun-shine came a - long with thee, and   swal-lows in the   air.

BEAUTIFUL BROWN EYES

Regi-Sound Program: 1
Rhythm: Waltz

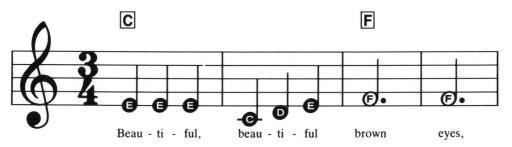

Beau - ti - ful, beau - ti - ful brown eyes,

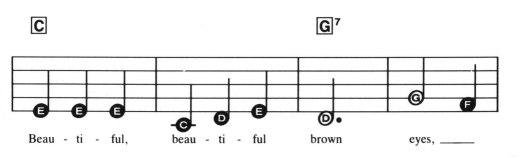

Beau - ti - ful, beau - ti - ful brown eyes, ____

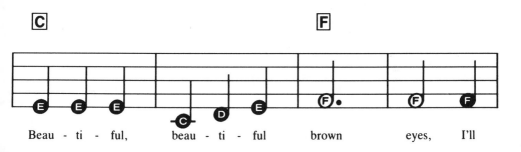

Beau - ti - ful, beau - ti - ful brown eyes, I'll

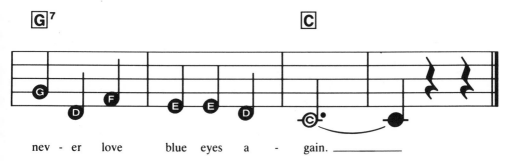

nev - er love blue eyes a - gain. ____

BLOW THE MAN DOWN

Regi-Sound Program: 2
Rhythm: Waltz

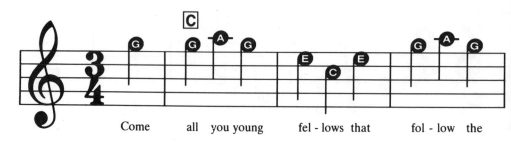

Come all you young fel - lows that fol - low the

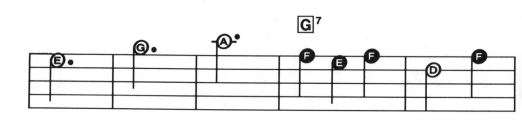

sea! Yeo! Ho! Blow the man down! And

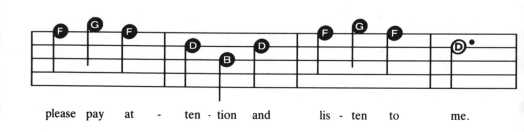

please pay at - ten - tion and lis - ten to me.

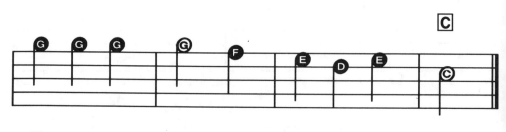

Give us some - time to blow the man down.

THE BLUE BELLS OF SCOTLAND

Regi-Sound Program: 9
Rhythm: Swing

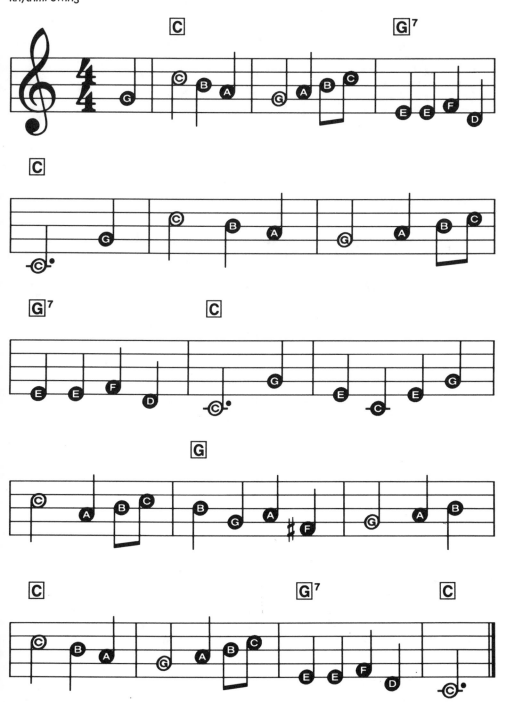

CAN CAN

Regi-Sound Program: 4
Rhythm: Polka or Fox Trot

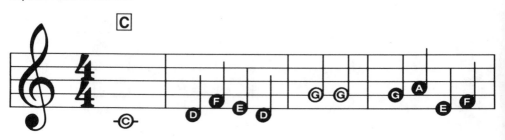

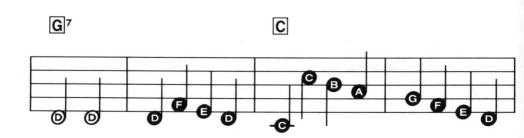

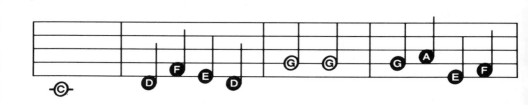

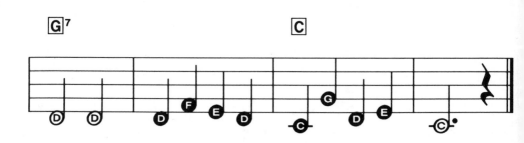

CARELESS LOVE

Regi-Sound Program: 7
Rhythm: Swing

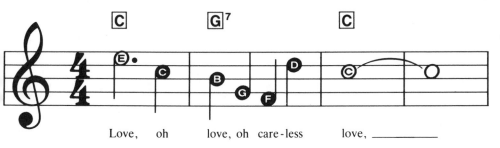

Love, oh love, oh care-less love, _____

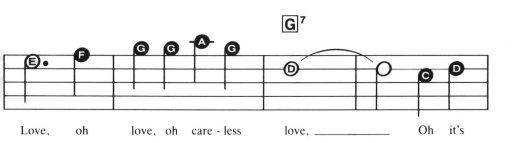

Love, oh love, oh care - less love, _____ Oh it's

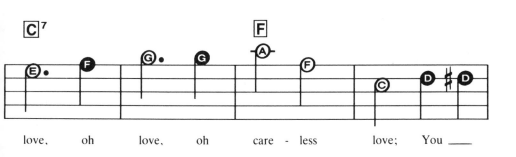

love, oh love, oh care - less love; You ___

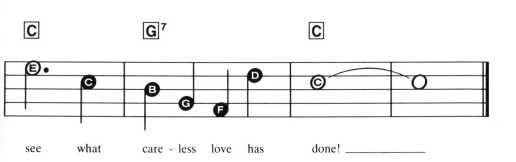

see what care - less love has done! _____

CHOPSTICKS

Regi-Sound Program: 8
Rhythm: Waltz

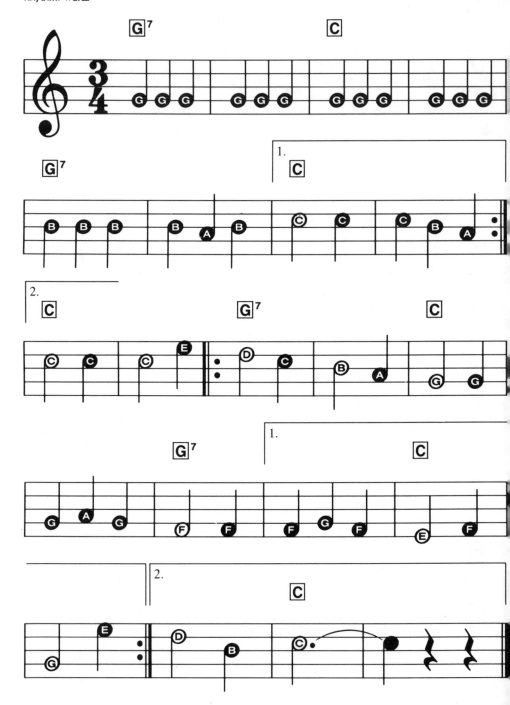

(OH, MY DARLING)
CLEMENTINE

Regi-Sound Program: 7
Rhythm: Waltz

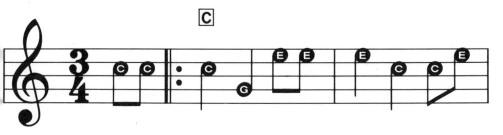

In a cav - ern in a can - yon, ex - ca -
dar - ling oh, my dar - ling oh, my

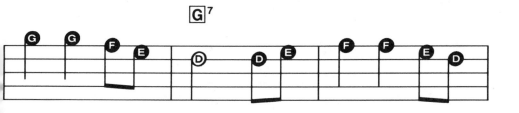

vat - ing for a mine dwelt a min - er, for - ty
dar - ling Clem - en - tine, you are lost and gone for -

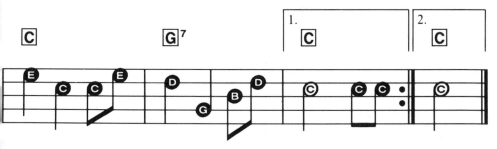

nin - er, and his daugh - ter, Clem-en - tine. Oh, my
ev - er dread-ful sor - ry, Clem-en - -tine.

COUNTRY GARDENS

Regi-Sound Program: 9
Rhythm: Swing

DARK EYES

Regi-Sound Program: 10
Rhythm: Waltz

FARMER IN THE DELL

Regi-Sound Program: 4
Rhythm: Waltz

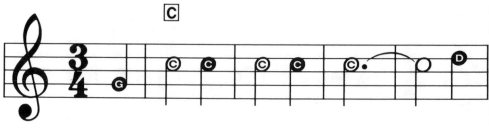

The   far - mer   in   the   dell _____ the

far   -   mer   in   the   dell _____

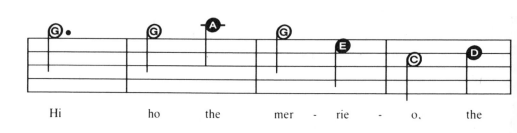

Hi   ho   the   mer - rie - o,   the

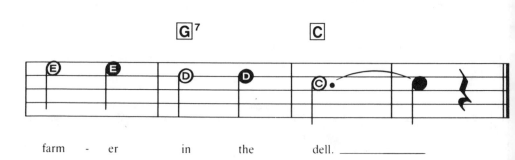

farm - er   in   the   dell. _____

GOOD NIGHT LADIES

Regi-Sound Program: 9
Rhythm: Swing

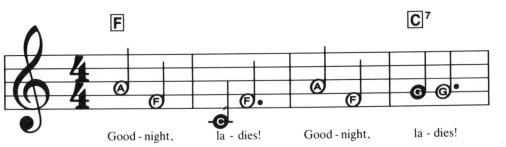

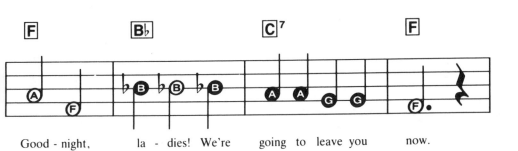

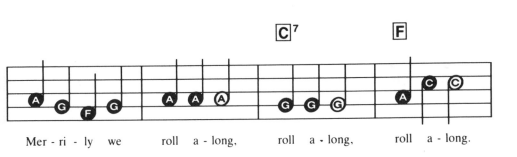

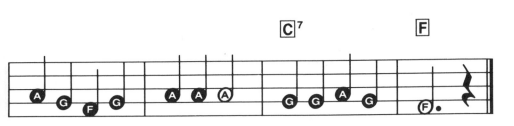

HAIL, HAIL, THE GANG'S ALL HERE

Regi-Sound Program: 8
Rhythm: Swing

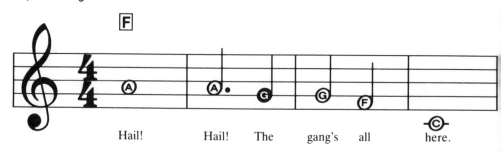

Hail!   Hail!   The   gang's   all   here.

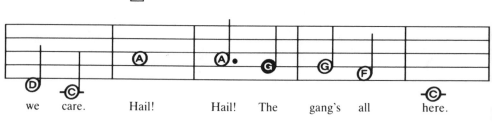

What   the   heck   do   we   care,   what   the   heck   do

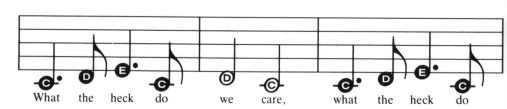

we   care.   Hail!   Hail!   The   gang's   all   here.

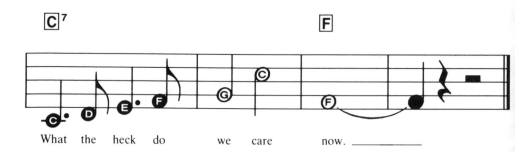

What   the   heck   do   we   care   now. _____

JULIDA POLKA

Regi-Sound Program: 4
Rhythm: Polka or Fox Trot

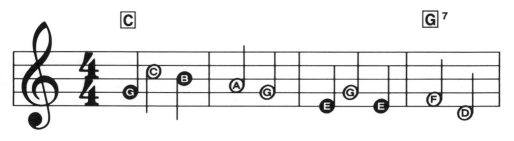

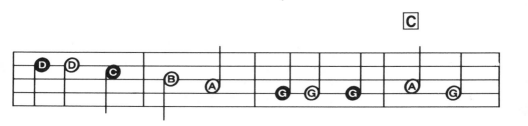

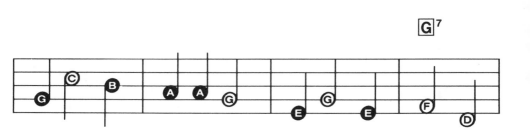

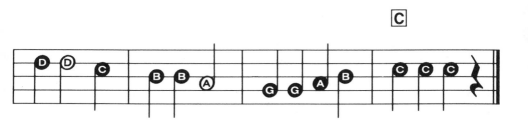

LIGHTLY ROW

Regi-Sound Program: 1
Rhythm: Swing

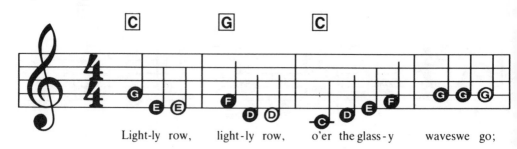

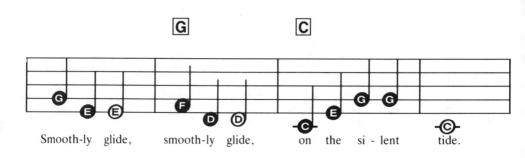

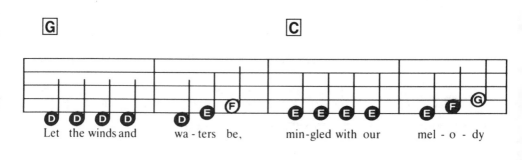

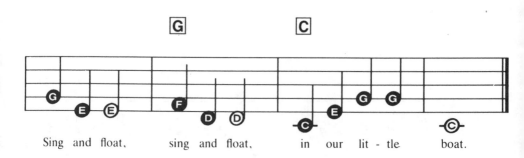

LULLABY

Regi-Sound Program: 1
Rhythm: Waltz

Go to sleep, now dear love, 'neath _ ros - es a -

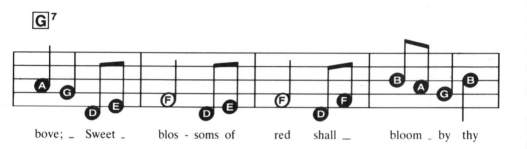

bove; _ Sweet _ blos - soms of red shall _ bloom _ by thy

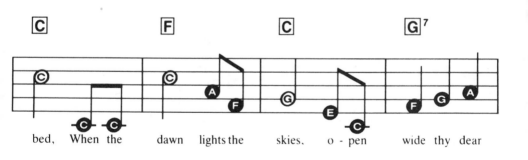

bed, When the dawn lights the skies, o - pen wide thy dear

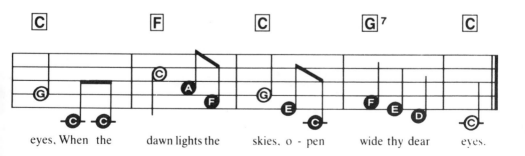

eyes, When the dawn lights the skies, o - pen wide thy dear eyes.

MARIANNE

Regi-Sound Program: 9
Rhythm: Swing

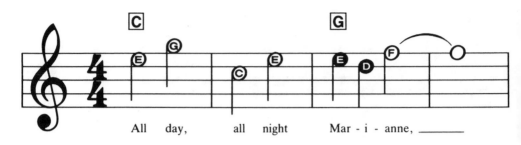

All day,   all night   Mar - i - anne, _____

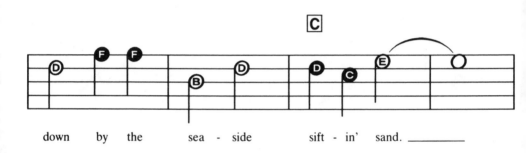

down   by   the   sea - side   sift - in' sand. _____

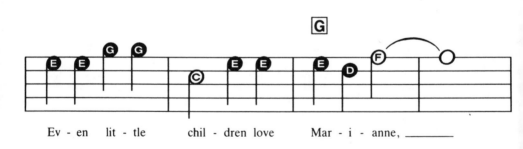

Ev - en   lit - tle   chil - dren love   Mar - i - anne, _____

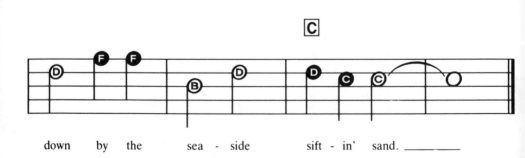

down   by   the   sea - side   sift - in' sand. _____

THE RED RIVER VALLEY

Regi-Sound Program: 5
Rhythm: Swing

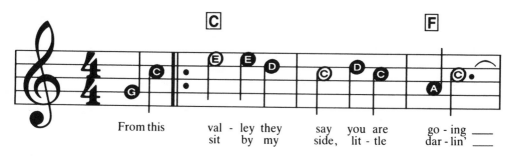

From this   val - ley they   say you are   go - ing ____
             sit   by my   side, lit - tle   dar - lin' ____

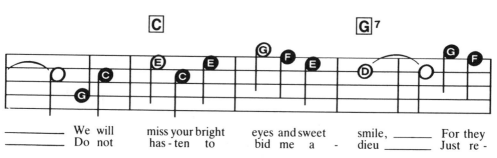

_____ We will   miss your bright   eyes and sweet   smile, _____ For they
_____ Do not   has - ten to   bid me a -   dieu _____ Just re -

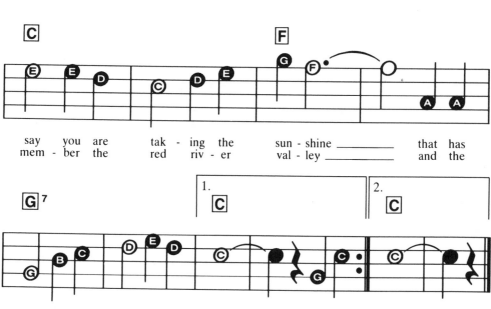

say   you are   tak - ing the   sun - shine _____   that has
mem - ber the   red riv - er   val - ley _____   and the

1.
2.

bright-ened our   path-way a   while. _____   Come and
cow - boy who   loves you so   true. _____

ROW ROW ROW YOUR BOAT

Regi-Sound Program: 2
Rhythm: Waltz

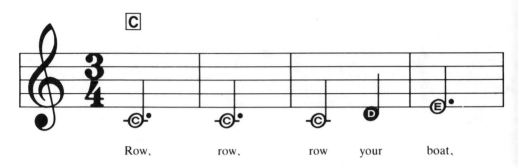

Row,   row,   row   your   boat,

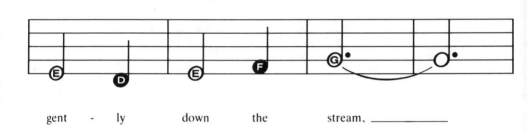

gent - ly   down   the   stream, _____

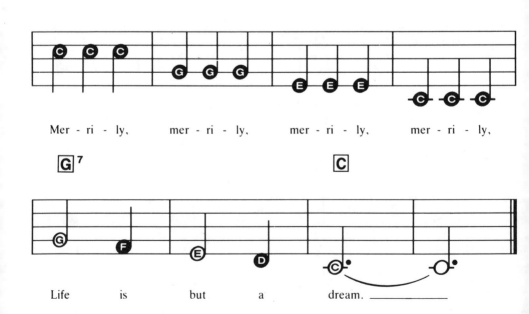

Mer - ri - ly,   mer - ri - ly,   mer - ri - ly,   mer - ri - ly,

Life   is   but   a   dream. _____

SCARBOROUGH FAIR

Regi-Sound Program: 6
Rhythm: Slow Waltz

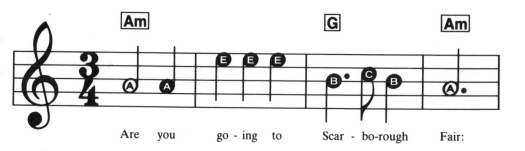

Are you go - ing to Scar - bo-rough Fair:

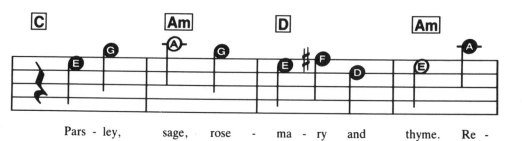

Pars - ley, sage, rose - ma - ry and thyme. Re -

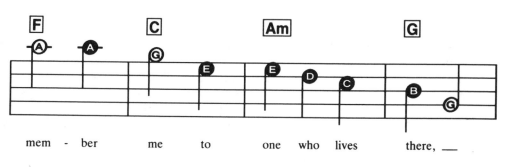

mem - ber me to one who lives there, ___

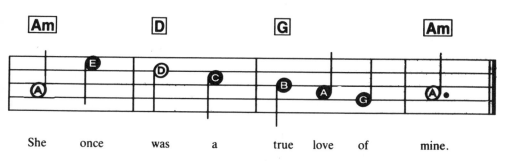

She once was a true love of mine.

THE SKATERS

Regi-Sound Program: 1
Rhythm: Waltz

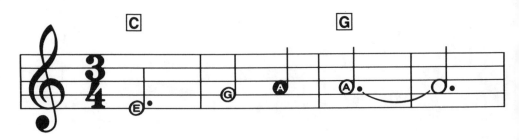

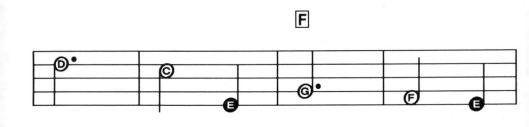

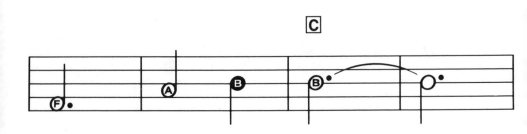

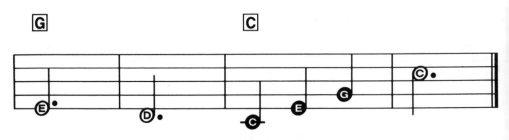

SKIP TO MY LOU

Regi-Sound Program: 4
Rhythm: Swing

Fly's in the but - ter - milk   shoo   fly   shoo,

Fly's   in   the   but - ter - milk   shoo   fly   shoo,

Fly's   in   the   but - ter - milk   shoo   fly   shoo

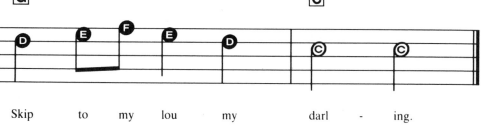

Skip   to   my   lou   my   darl - ing.

SPRING SONG, OP. 68 #15

Regi-Sound Program: 1
Rhythm: Fox Trot or Swing

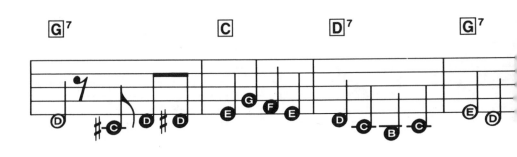

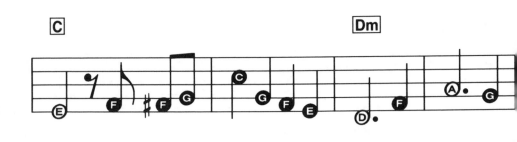

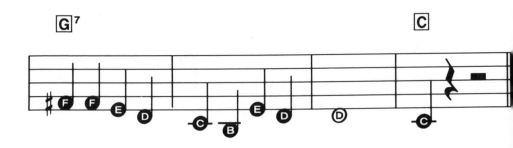

SWEET ADELINE
(a/k/a YOU'RE THE FLOWER OF MY HEART, SWEET ADELINE)

Regi-Sound Program: 7
Rhythm: Slow Swing

THIS OLD MAN

Regi-Sound Program: 4
Rhythm: March

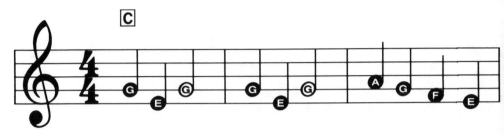

1. This old man, he played one. He played knick, knack

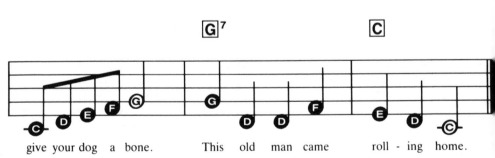

on his thumb With a knick, knack, pat - ty whack,

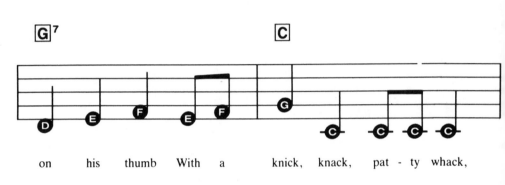

give your dog a bone. This old man came roll - ing home.

2. This old man, he played two. He played knick, knack, on my shoe
With a knick, knack, patty whack, give your dog a bone.
This old man came rolling home.

3. This old man, he played three. He played knick, knack, on my knee
With a knick, knack, patty whack, give your dog a bone.
This old man came rolling home.

4. This old man, he played four. He played knick, knack, on this door
With a knick, knack, patty whack, give your dog a bone.
This old man came rolling home.

TOREADOR SONG

Regi-Sound Program: 4
Rhythm: March

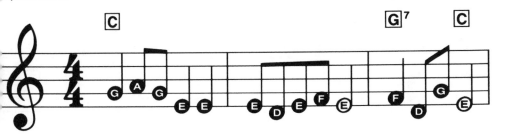

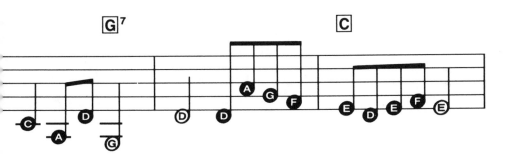

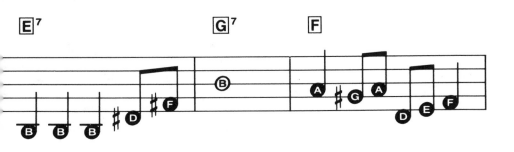

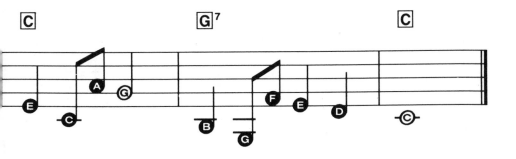

TWINKLE TWINKLE LITTLE STAR

Regi-Sound Program: 9
Rhythm: Swing

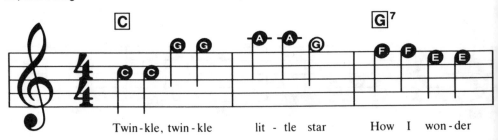

Twin - kle, twin - kle lit - tle star How I won - der

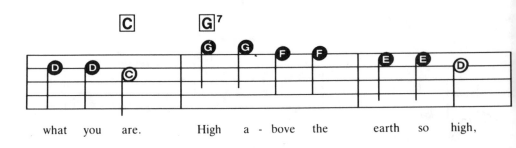

what you are. High a - bove the earth so high,

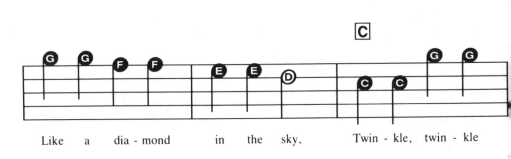

Like a dia - mond in the sky, Twin - kle, twin - kle

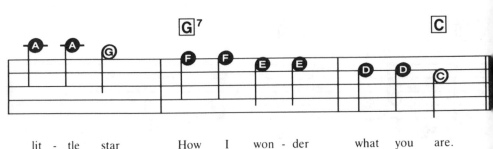

lit - tle star How I won - der what you are.

WHEN THE SAINTS GO MARCHING IN

Regi-Sound Program: 4
Rhythm: March

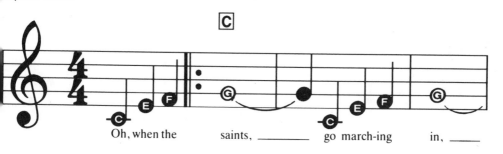

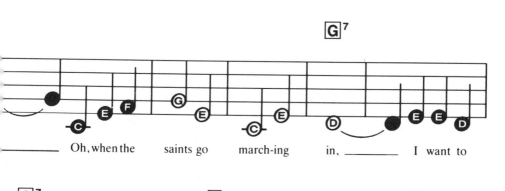

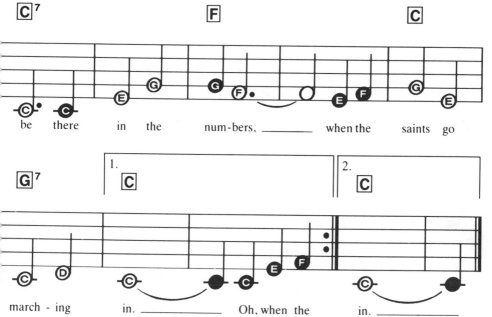

BILL BAILEY, WON'T YOU PLEASE COME HOME

Regi-Sound Program: 4
Rhythm: Swing

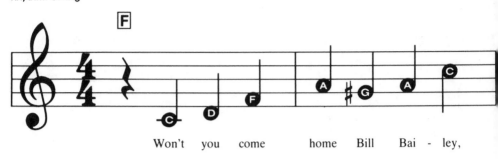

Won't you come home Bill Bai - ley,

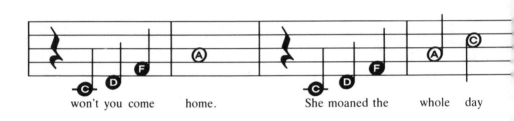

won't you come home. She moaned the whole day

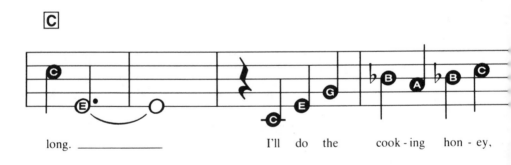

long. _____ I'll do the cook - ing hon - ey,

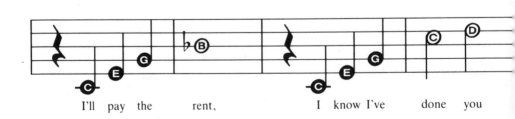

I'll pay the rent, I know I've done you

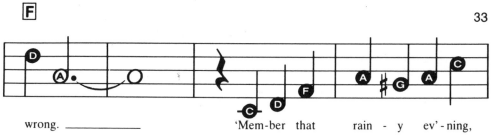

wrong. _____ 'Mem-ber that rain - y ev' - ning,

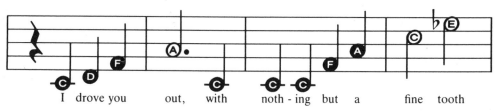

I drove you out, with noth - ing but a fine tooth

comb? _____ I know I'm to blame, well

ain't that a shame, Bill Bai - ley, won't you

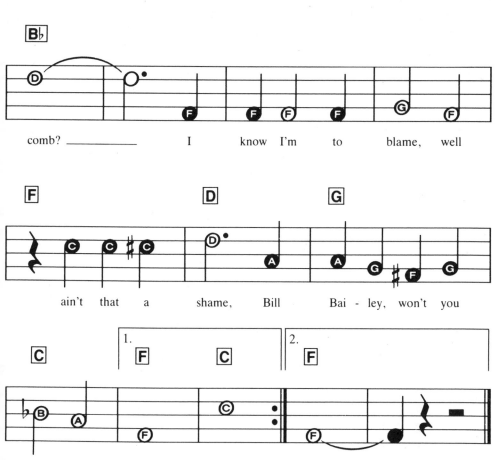

please come home? _____ home? _____

MY BONNIE LIES OVER THE OCEAN

Regi-Sound Program: 4
Rhythm: Waltz

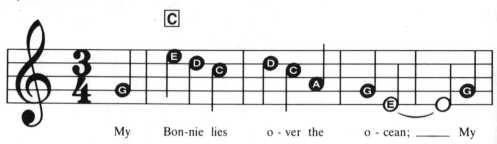

My Bon-nie lies o - ver the o - cean; _____ My

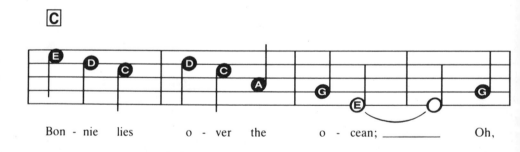

Bon - nie lies o - ver the sea. _____ My

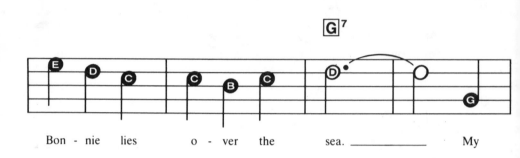

Bon - nie lies o - ver the o - cean; _____ Oh,

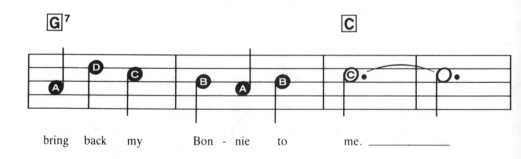

bring back my Bon - nie to me. _____

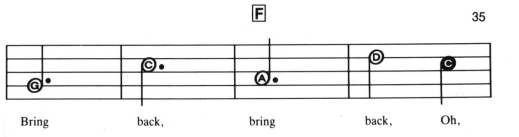

Bring　　　　back,　　　　bring　　　　back,　　　Oh,

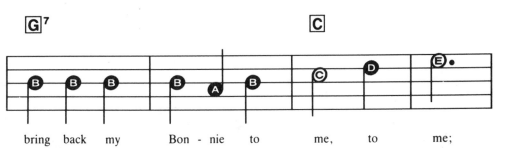

bring　back　my　Bon - nie　to　me,　to　me;

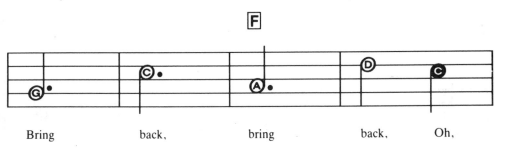

Bring　　　　back,　　　　bring　　　　back,　　　Oh,

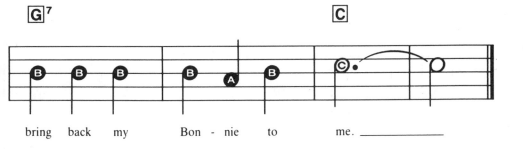

bring　back　my　Bon - nie　to　me. _____

CIELITO LINDO

Regi-Sound Program: 7
Rhythm: Waltz

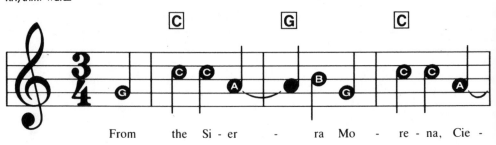

From the Si - er - ra Mo - re - na, Cie -

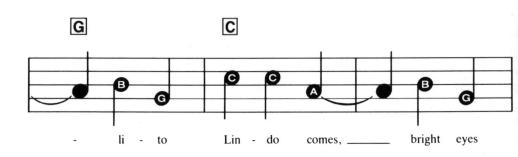

- li - to Lin - do comes, _____ bright eyes

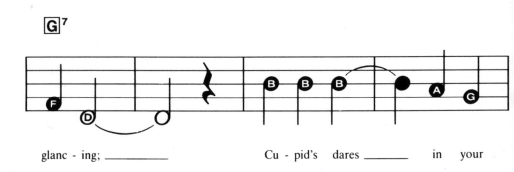

glanc - ing; _____ Cu - pid's dares _____ in your

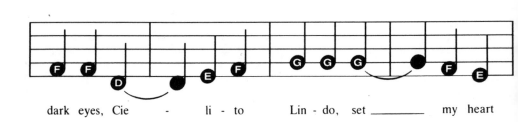

dark eyes, Cie - li - to Lin - do, set _____ my heart

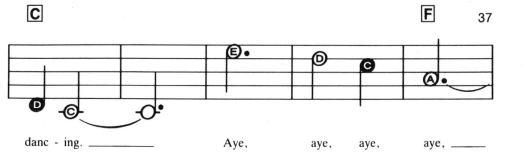

danc - ing. _____ Aye, aye, aye, aye, _____

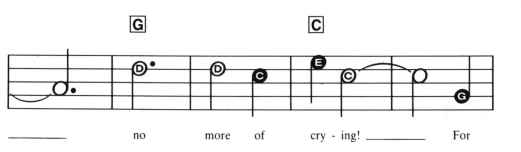

_____ no more of cry - ing! _____ For

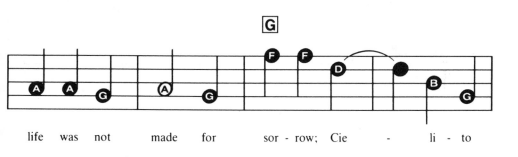

life was not made for sor - row; Cie - li - to

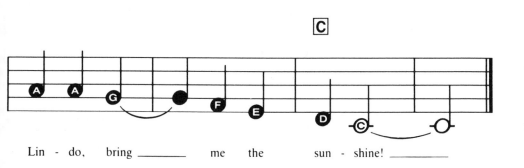

Lin - do, bring _____ me the sun - shine! _____

CLAIR DE LUNE

Regi-Sound Program: 1
Rhythm: 8 Beat

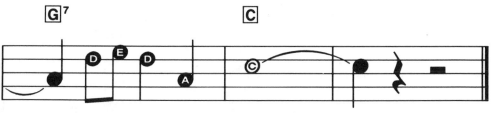

COME BACK TO SORRENTO

Regi-Sound Program: 3
Rhythm: Waltz

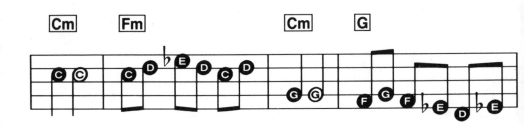

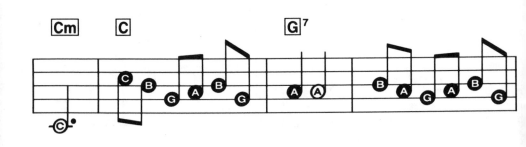

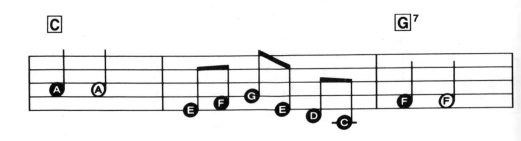

A BICYCLE BUILT FOR TWO
(a/k/a DAISY BELL)

Regi-Sound Program: 8
Rhythm: Waltz

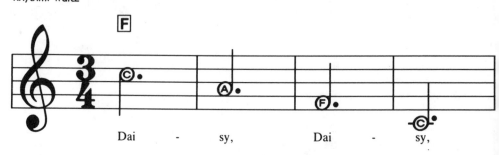

Dai - sy, Dai - sy,

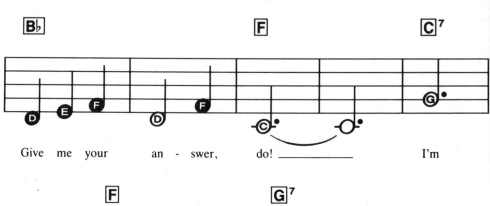

Give me your an - swer, do! _____ I'm

half cra - zy, all for the love of

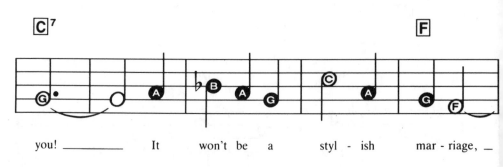

you! _____ It won't be a styl - ish mar - riage, _

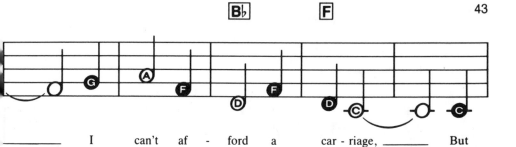

I can't af - ford a car - riage, _____ But

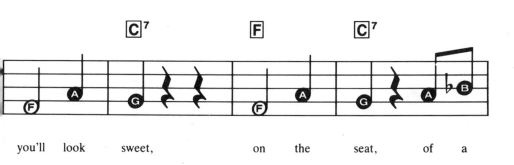

you'll look sweet, on the seat, of a

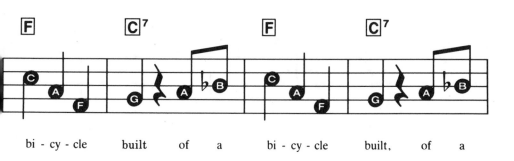

bi - cy - cle built of a bi - cy - cle built, of a

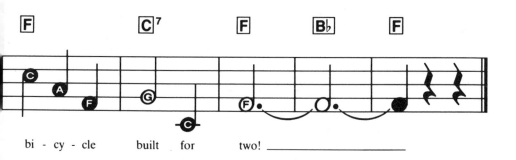

bi - cy - cle built for two! _____

DOWN IN THE VALLEY

Regi-Sound Program: 1
Rhythm: Waltz

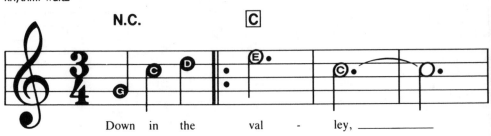

Down in the val - ley, _____

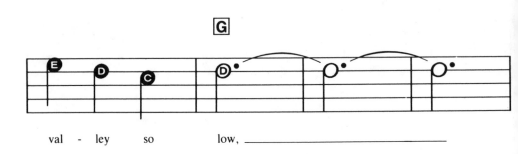

val - ley so low, _____

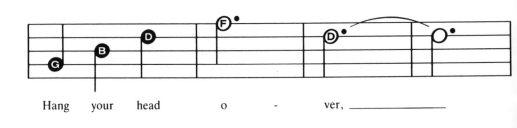

Hang your head o - ver, _____

hear the wind blow. _____ Hear the wind

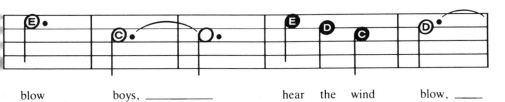

blow   boys, _____   hear the wind   blow, _____

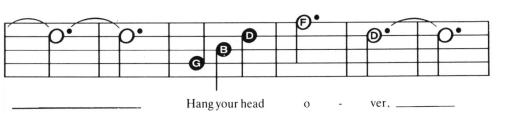

_____   Hang your head   o - ver, _____

1.
C

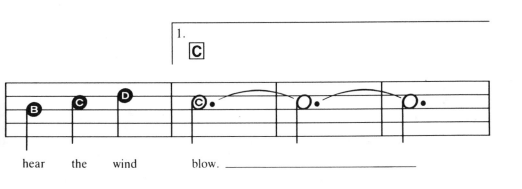

hear   the   wind   blow. _____

2.
C

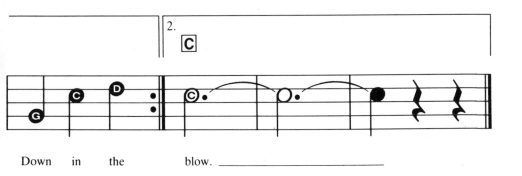

Down   in   the   blow. _____

DOWN BY THE OLD MILL STREAM

Regi-Sound Program: 4
Rhythm: Swing

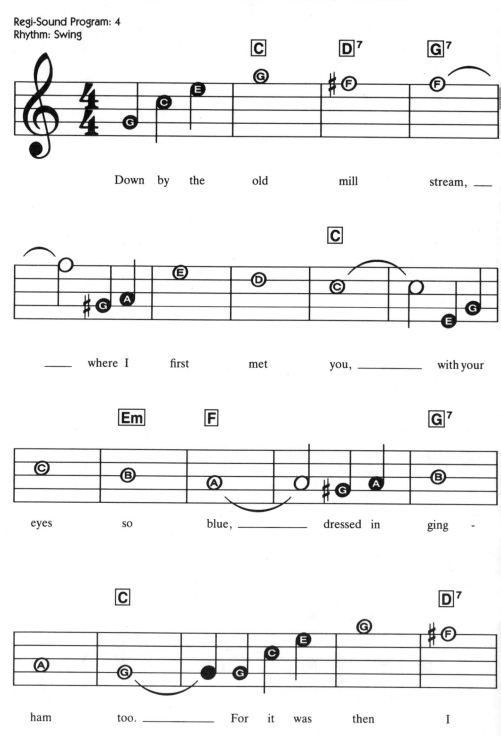

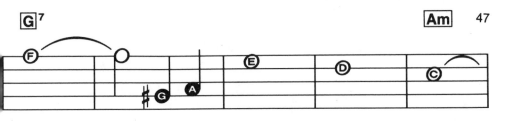

knew _____ that you loved me true, _____

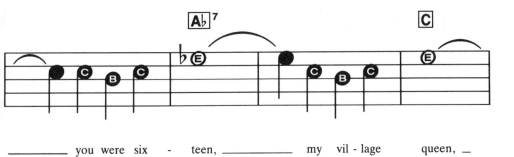

_____ you were six - teen, _____ my vil - lage queen, _

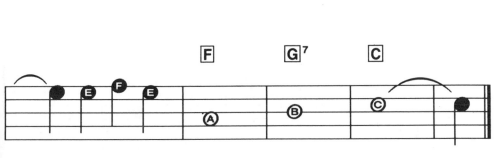

_____ down by the old mill stream. _____

FASCINATION
(VALSE TZIGANE)

Regi-Sound Program: 9
Rhythm: Waltz

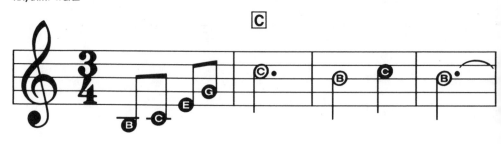

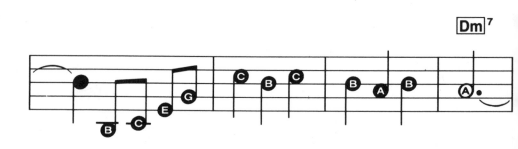

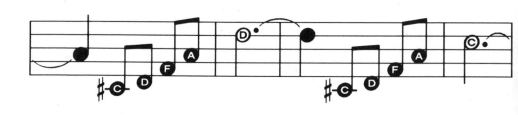

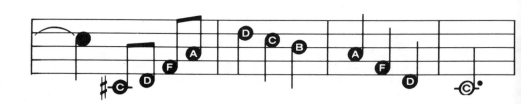

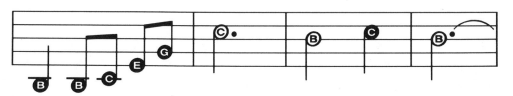

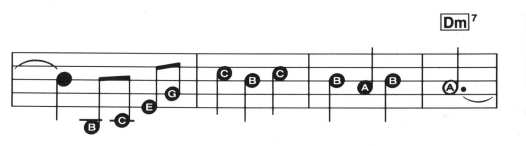

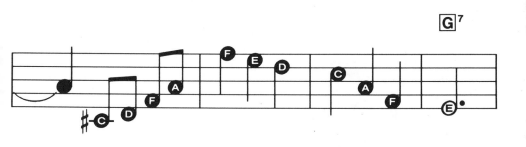

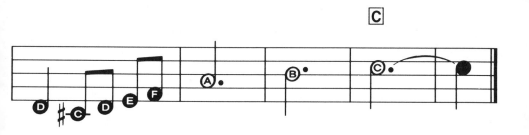

FRANKIE AND JOHNNY

Regi-Sound Program: 4
Rhythm: Swing

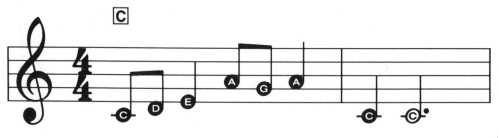

Frank - ie and John - ny were lov - ers,

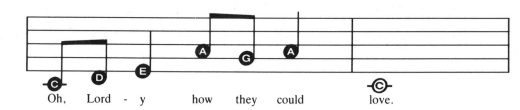

Oh, Lord - y how they could love.

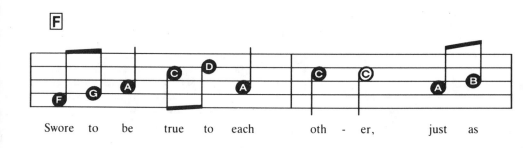

Swore to be true to each oth - er, just as

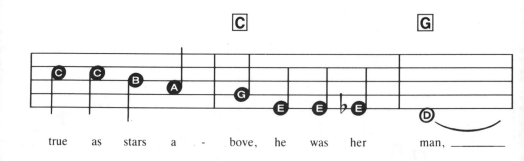

true as stars a - bove, he was her man, _____

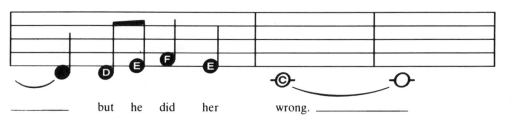

but he did her wrong. _____

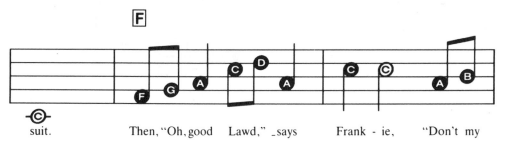

Frank-ie and John-ny went walk-ing, John in his brand _ new

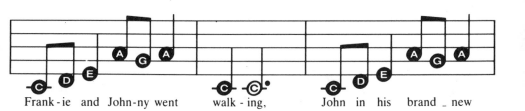

suit. Then, "Oh, good Lawd," _says Frank-ie, "Don't my

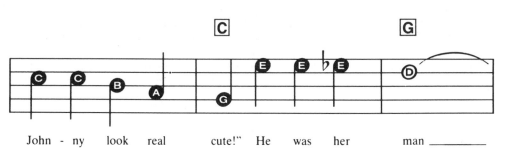

John-ny look real cute!" He was her man _____

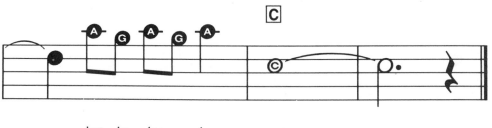

_____ but he done _ her wrong. _____

HUNGARIAN DANCE NO. 5

Regi-Sound Program: 6
Rhythm: March or Polka

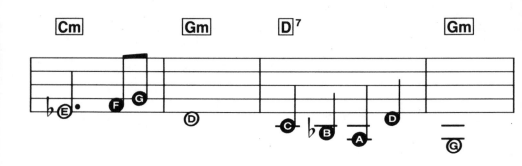

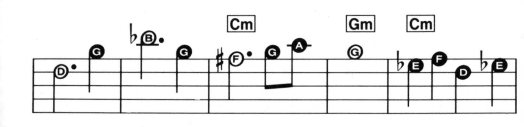

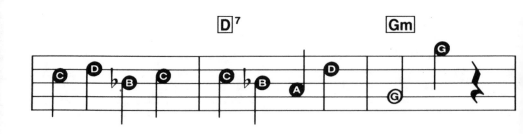

I WONDER WHO'S KISSING HER NOW

Regi-Sound Program: 9
Rhythm: Waltz

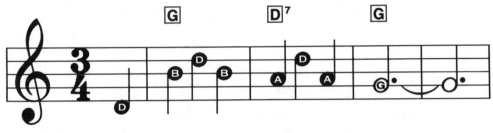

I won-der who's kiss-ing her now, _____

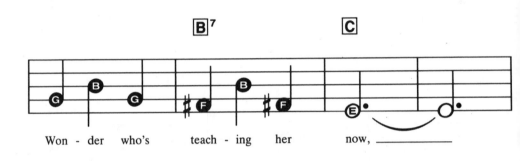

Won - der who's teach - ing her now, _____

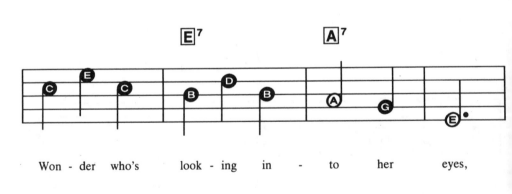

Won - der who's look - ing in - to her eyes,

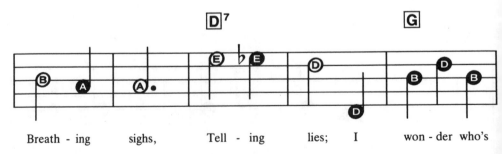

Breath - ing sighs, Tell - ing lies; I won - der who's

buy - ing the wine, _____ For lips that I used to call

mine, _____ Won - der if she ev - er tells him of

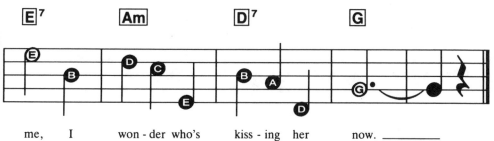

me, I won - der who's kiss - ing her now. _____

IDA, SWEET AS APPLE CIDER

Regi-Sound Program: 4
Rhythm: Swing

I - da! _____ Sweet as ap - ple ci - der, __

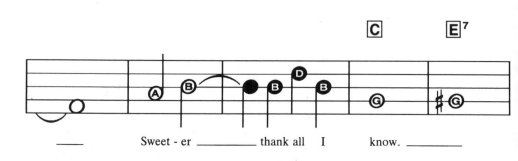

____ Sweet - er _____ thank all I know. _____

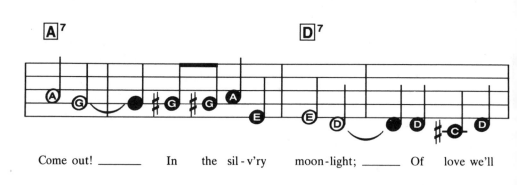

Come out! _____ In the sil - v'ry moon-light; _____ Of love we'll

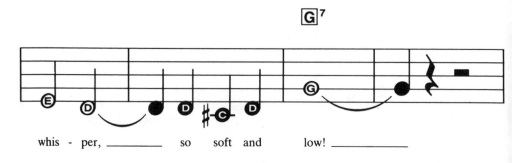

whis - per, _____ so soft and low! _____

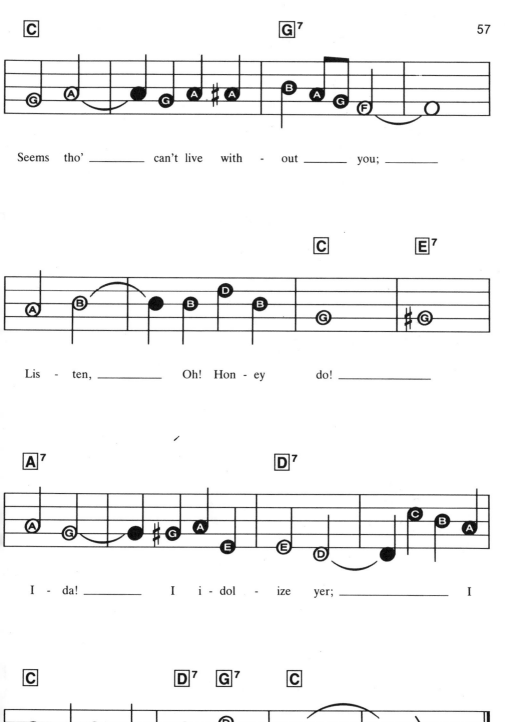

IN THE GOOD OLD SUMMERTIME

Regi-Sound Program: 4
Rhythm: Waltz

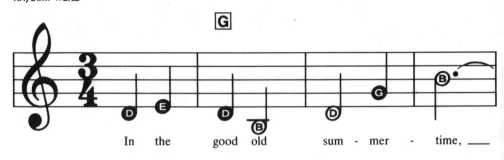

In the good old sum - mer - time, ___

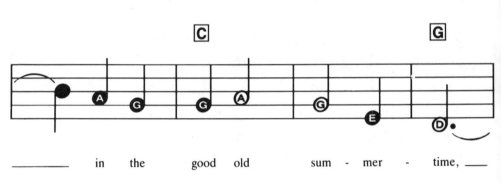

___ in the good old sum - mer - time, ___

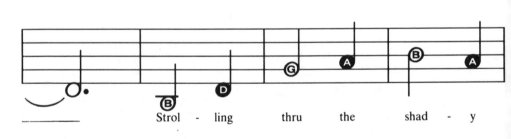

___ Strol - ling thru the shad - y

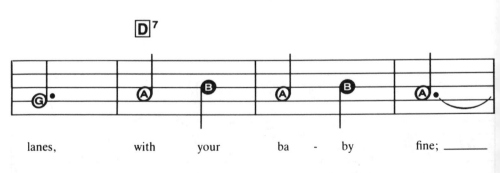

lanes, with your ba - by fine; ___

G

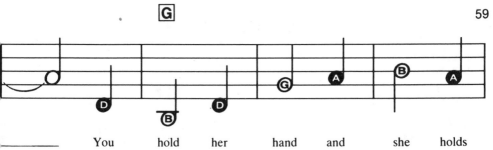

You hold her hand and she holds

C   G

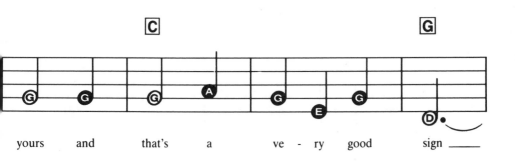

yours and that's a ve - ry good sign _____

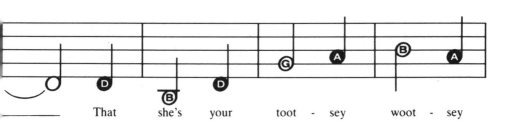

That she's your toot - sey woot - sey

C   D⁷   G

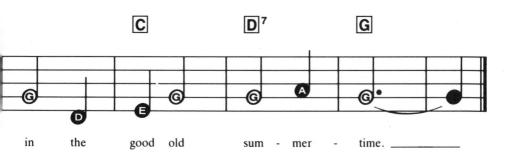

in the good old sum - mer - time. _____

IN THE GLOAMING

Regi-Sound Program: 1
Rhythm: Swing

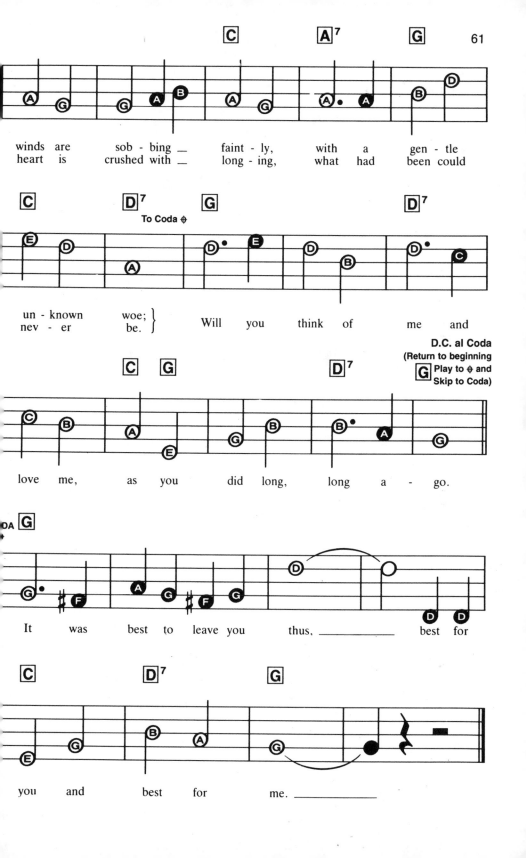

JEANNIE

Regi-Sound Program: 8
Rhythm: Swing

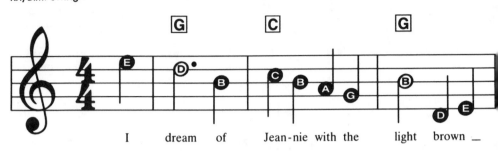

I dream of Jean-nie with the light brown _

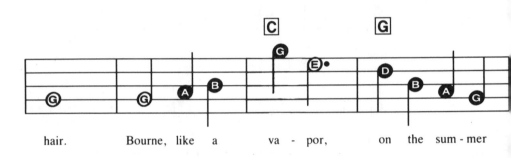

hair. Bourne, like a va - por, on the sum - mer

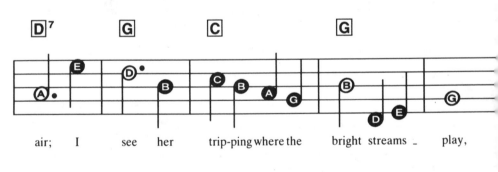

air; I see her trip-ping where the bright streams _ play,

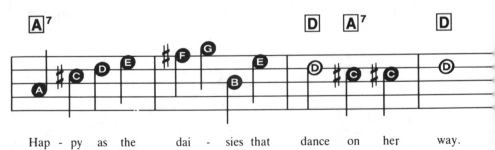

Hap - py as the dai - sies that dance on her way.

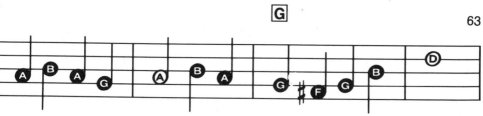

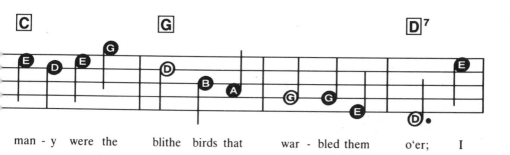

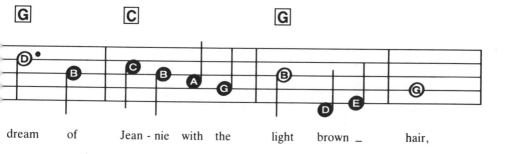

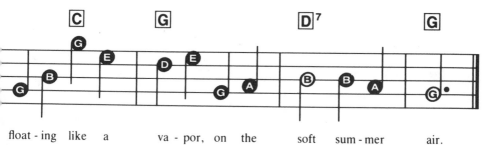

LA PALOMA

Regi-Sound Program: 9
Rhythm: Latin or Bossa Nova

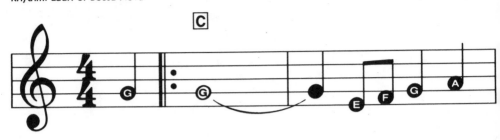

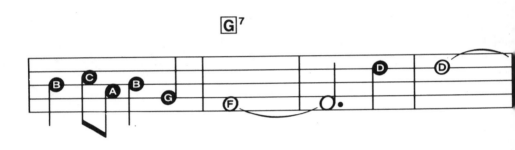

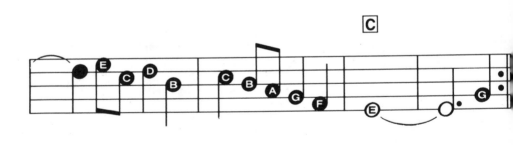

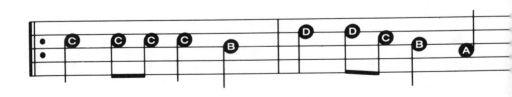

LAVENDER'S BLUE

Regi-Sound Program: 8
Rhythm: Swing

LET ME CALL YOU SWEETHEART

Regi-Sound Program: 7
Rhythm: Slow Waltz

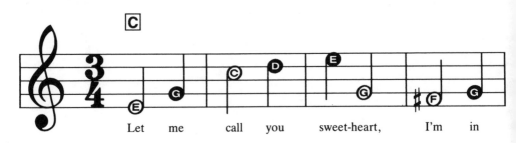

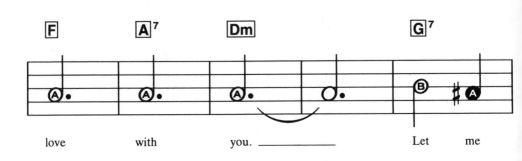

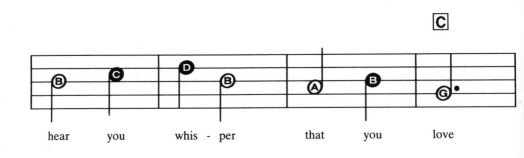

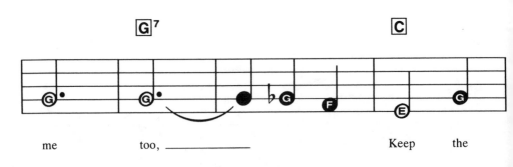

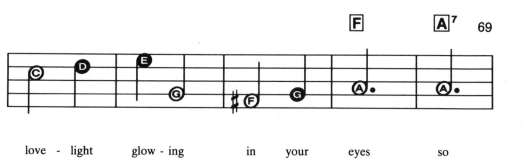

love - light glow - ing in your eyes so

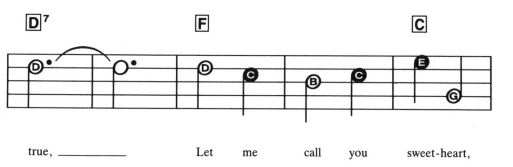

true, _____ Let me call you sweet-heart,

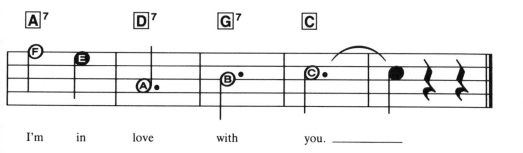

I'm in love with you. _____

LONDONDERRY AIR

Regi-Sound Program: 1
Rhythm: Swing

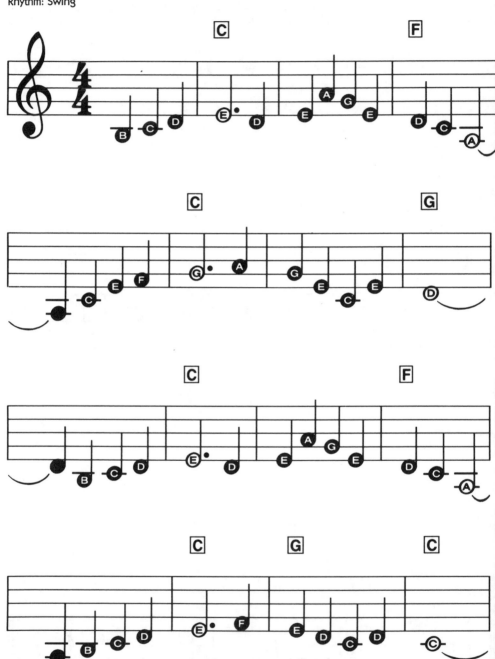

71

MAORI FAREWELL SONG

Regi-Sound Program: 1
Rhythm: Waltz

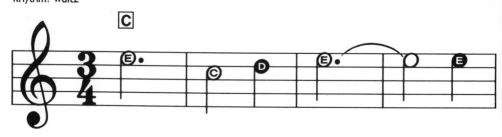

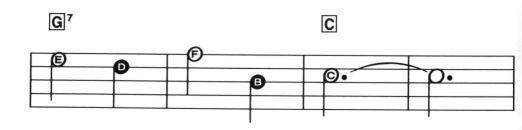

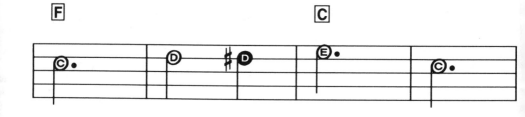

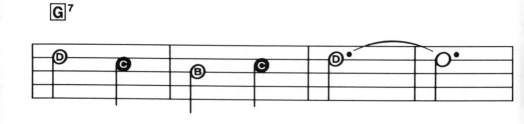

73

MEET ME TONIGHT IN DREAMLAND

Regi-Sound Program: 1
Rhythm: Waltz

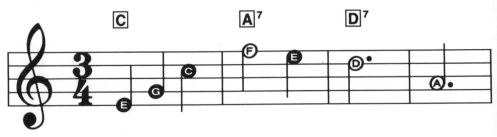

Meet me to - night in dream - land,

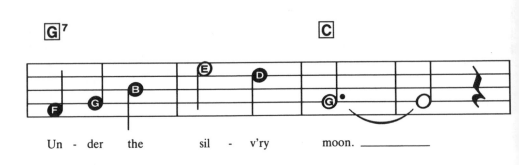

Un - der the sil - v'ry moon. _____

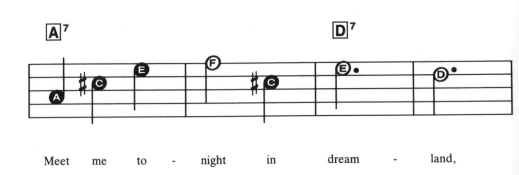

Meet me to - night in dream - land,

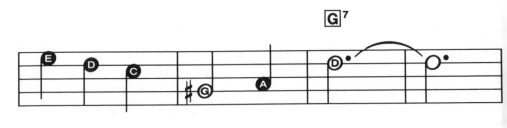

Where love's sweet ro - ses bloom. _____

MY WILD IRISH ROSE

Regi-Sound Program: 4
Rhythm: Waltz

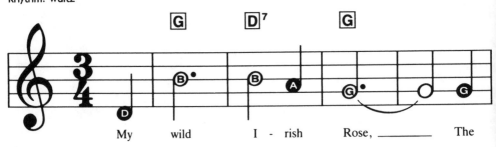

My   wild   I - rish   Rose, _____   The

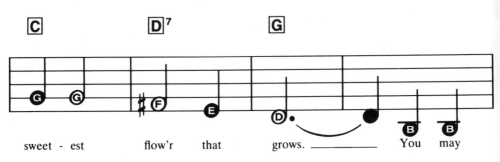

sweet - est   flow'r   that   grows. _____   You   may

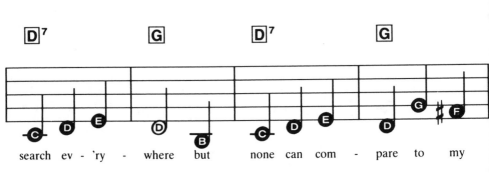

search   ev - 'ry - where   but   none   can   com - pare   to   my

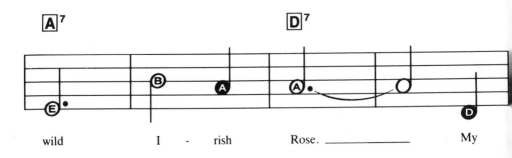

wild   I - rish   Rose. _____   My

MY GAL SAL

Regi-Sound Program: 4
Rhythm: Swing

Words and Music by
PAUL DRESSER

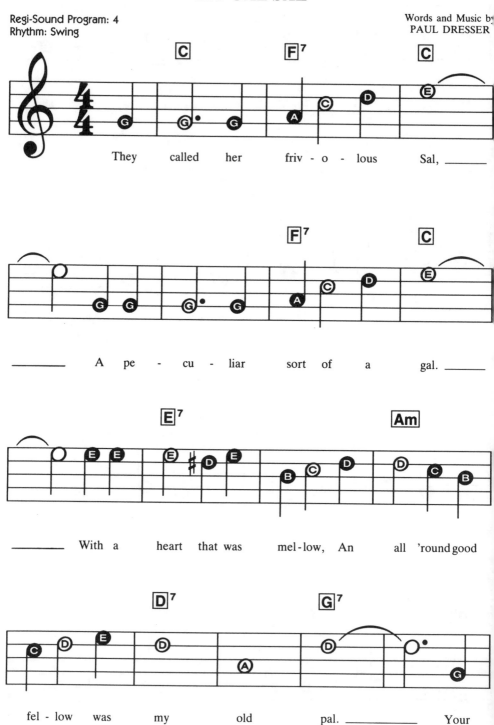

'O SOLE MIO

Regi-Sound Program: 9
Rhythm: Latin or Beguine

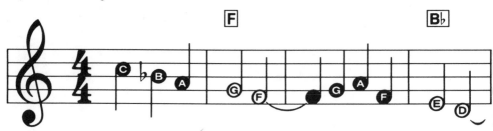

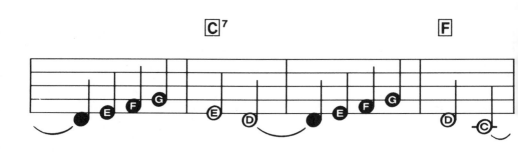

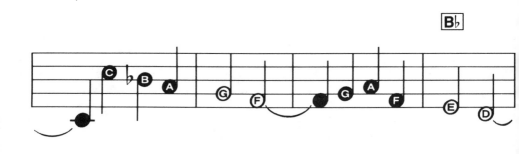

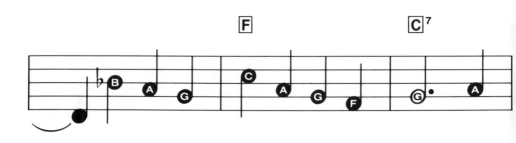

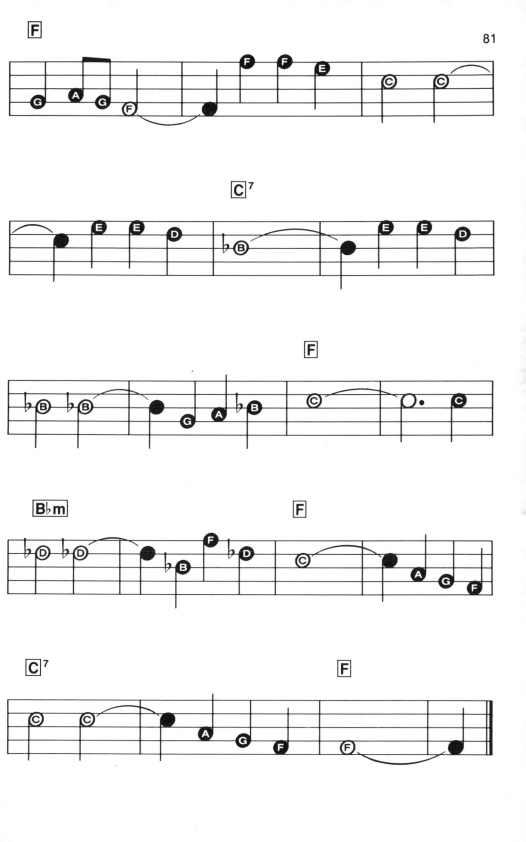

OH! SUSANNA

Regi-Sound Program: 8
Rhythm: Swing

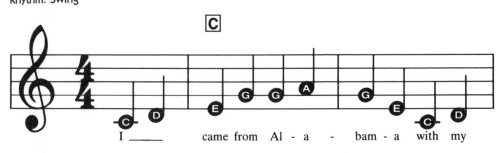

I _____ came from Al - a - bam - a with my

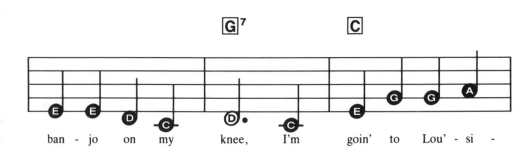

ban - jo on my knee, I'm goin' to Lou' - si -

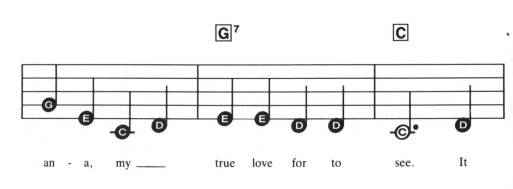

an - a, my _____ true love for to see. It

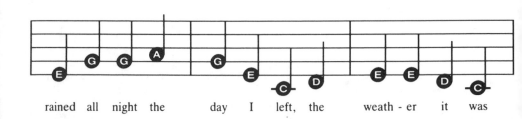

rained all night the day I left, the weath - er it was

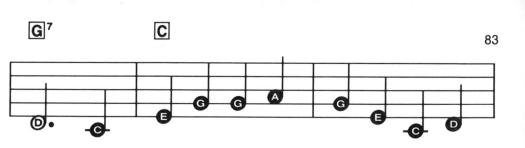

dry, the sun so hot I froze to death, Su -

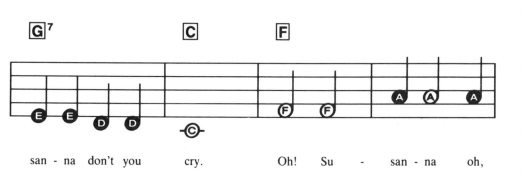

san - na don't you cry. Oh! Su - san - na oh,

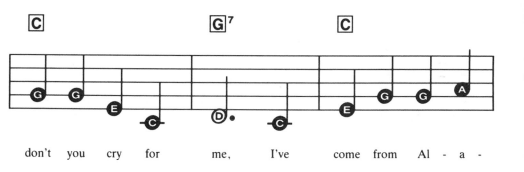

don't you cry for me, I've come from Al - a -

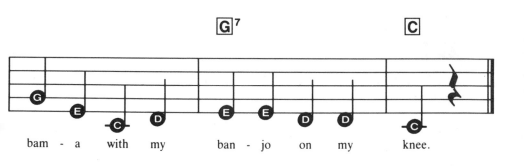

bam - a with my ban - jo on my knee.

ON A SUNDAY AFTERNOON

Regi-Sound Program: 4
Rhythm: Waltz

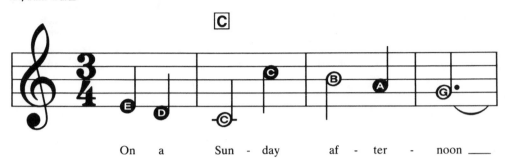

On a Sun - day af - ter - noon ___

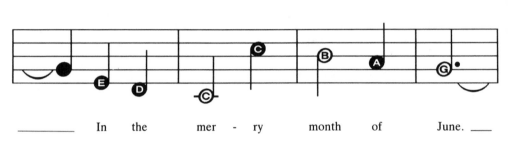

___ In the mer - ry month of June. ___

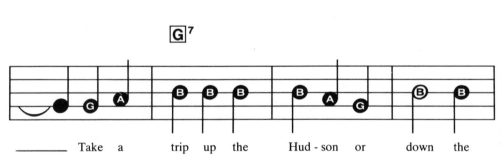

___ Take a trip up the Hud - son or down the

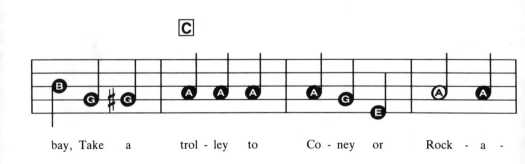

bay, Take a trol - ley to Co - ney or Rock - a -

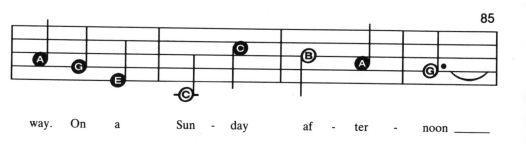

way. On a Sun - day af - ter - noon _____

F

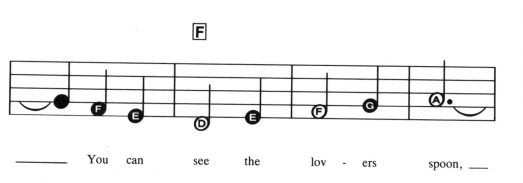

_____ You can see the lov - ers spoon, ___

G⁷

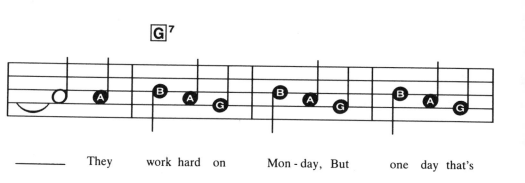

_____ They work hard on Mon - day, But one day that's

C

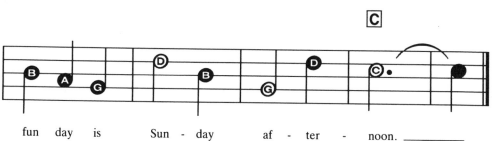

fun day is Sun - day af - ter - noon. _____

PUT YOUR ARMS AROUND ME, HONEY

Regi-Sound Program: 9
Rhythm: Swing

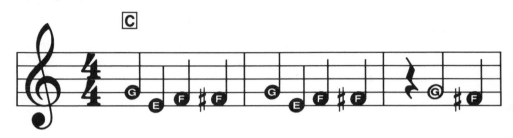

Put your arms a - round me, hon - ey,　　　hold　me

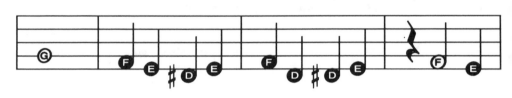

tight,　Hud - dle　up and　cud - dle　up with　　　all　your

might.　Oh,　　babe,　　won't　you　roll　dem　　eyes,

Eyes　　that　　　I　just　i - dol - ize.

When they look at me, my heart be - gins to float,

G⁷

Then it starts a - rock - in' like a mo - tor boat.

C

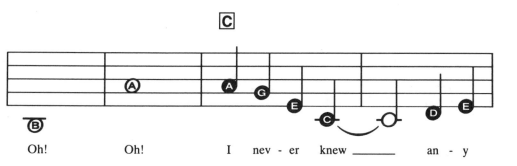

Oh! Oh! I nev - er knew _____ an - y

G⁷   **C**

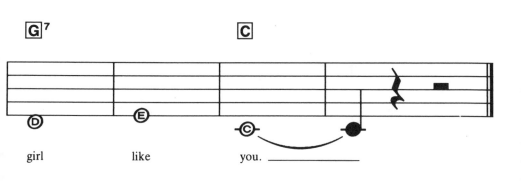

girl like you. _____

ROCK-A-BYE, BABY

Regi-Sound Program: 3
Rhythm: Waltz

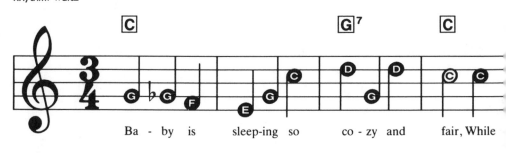

Ba - by is sleep-ing so co - zy and fair, While

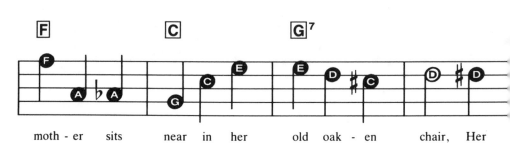

moth - er sits near in her old oak - en chair, Her

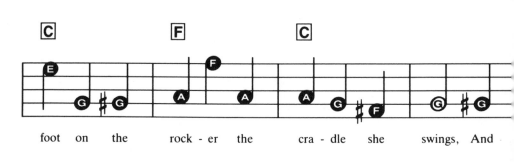

foot on the rock - er the cra - dle she swings, And

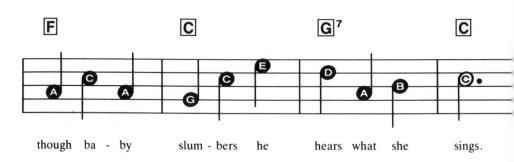

though ba - by slum - bers he hears what she sings.

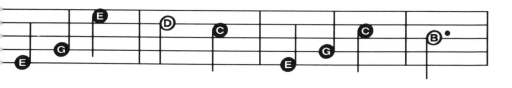

Rock - a - bye,   ba - by,   on   the   tree   top,

F   **C**

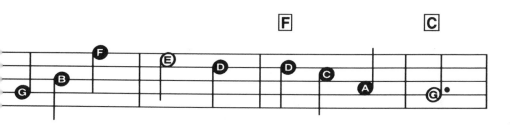

When   the   wind   blows   the   cra - dle   will   rock.

G

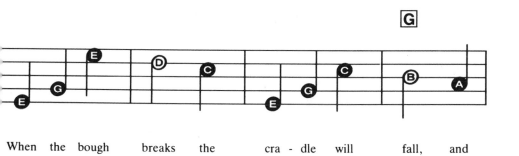

When   the   bough   breaks   the   cra - dle   will   fall,   and

C   **G**⁷   **C**

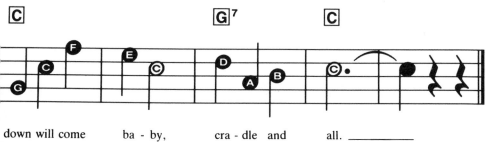

down will come   ba - by,   cra - dle and   all. _____

SANTA LUCIA

Regi-Sound Program: 9
Rhythm: Waltz

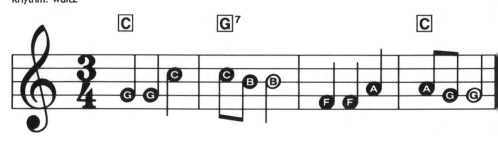

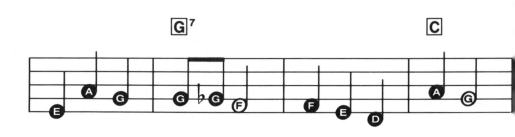

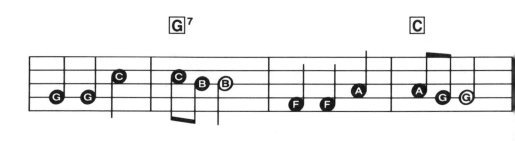

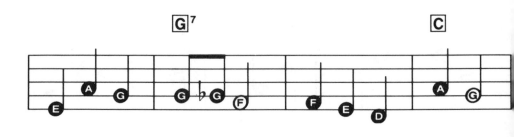

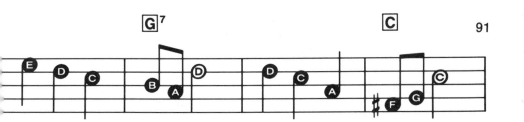

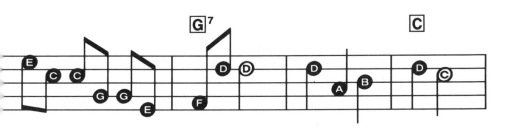

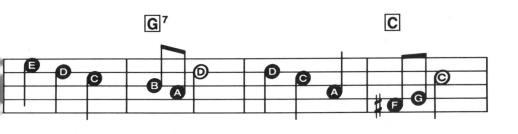

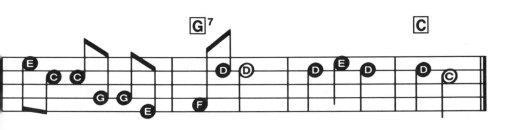

SCHOOL DAYS
(a/k/a WHEN WE WERE A COUPLE OF KIDS)

Regi-Sound Program: 7
Rhythm: Waltz

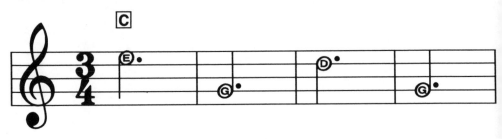

School   days,   School   days,

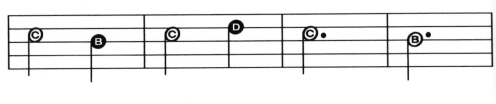

dear   old   gold - en   rule   days.

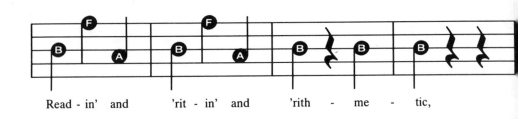

Read - in' and   'rit - in' and   'rith - me - tic,

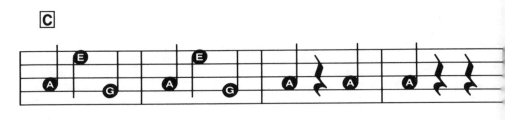

Taught to the   tune of a   hick - 'ry   stick.

You were my queen in cal - i - co,

I was your bash - ful bare - foot beau. And you

wrote on my slate, "I love you, Joe," When

we were a cou - ple of kids. _____

SIDEWALKS OF NEW YORK

Regi-Sound Program: 4
Rhythm: Waltz

TAKE ME OUT TO THE BALL GAME

Regi-Sound Program: 6
Rhythm: Waltz

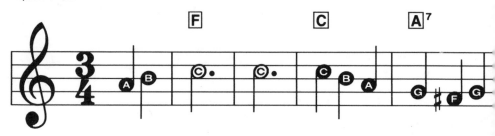

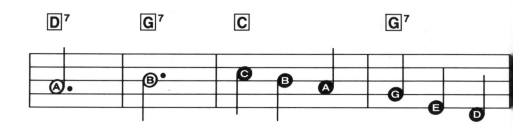

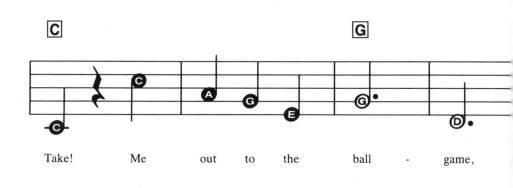

Take!   Me   out   to   the   ball - game,

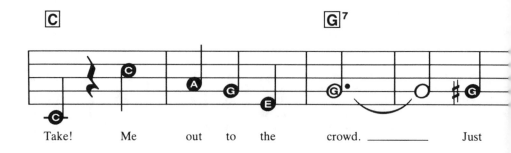

Take!   Me   out   to   the   crowd. _____ Just

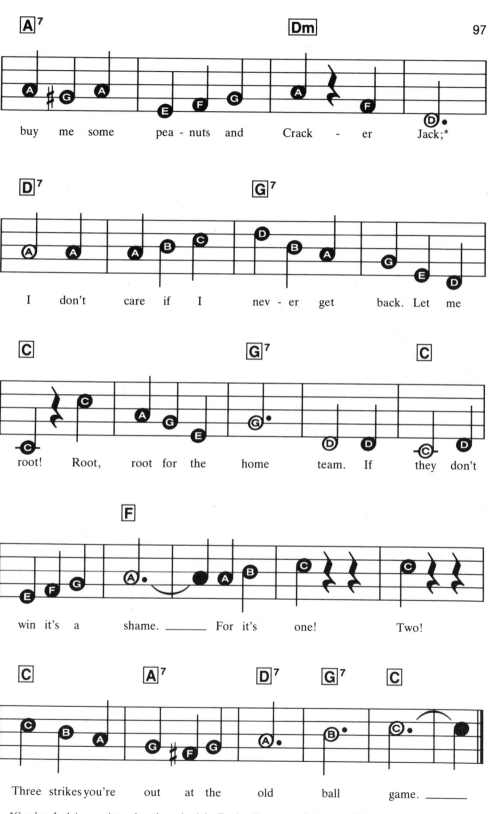

*Cracker Jack is a registered trademark of the Borden Company, Columbus, Ohio

TALES FROM THE VIENNA WOODS

Regi-Sound Program: 4
Rhythm: Waltz

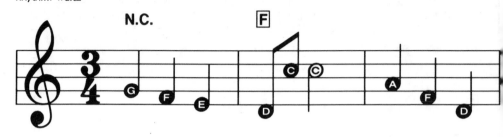

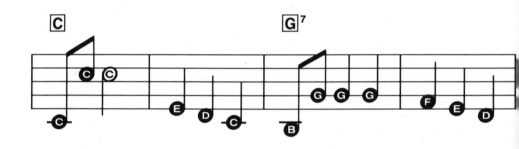

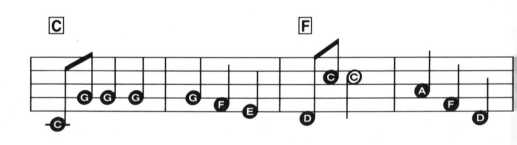

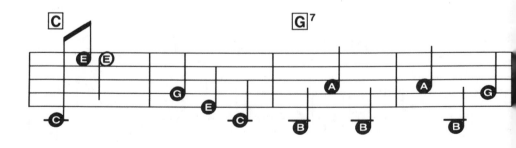

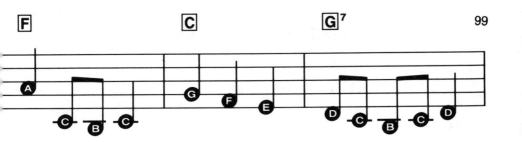

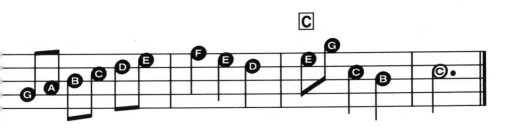

WALTZ OF THE FLOWERS

Regi-Sound Program: 1
Rhythm: Waltz

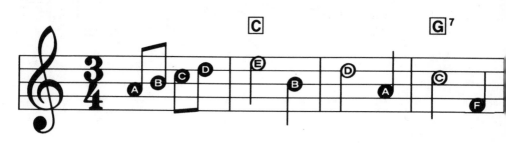

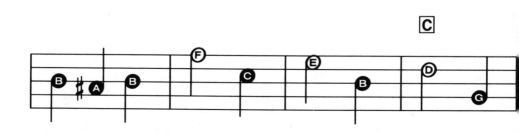

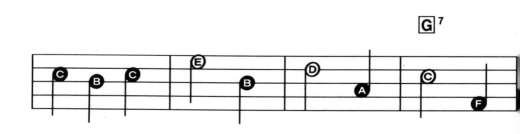

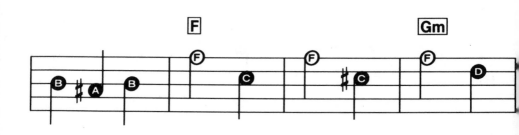

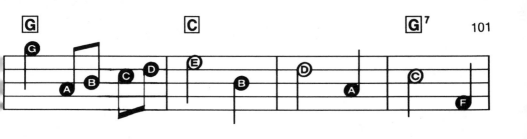

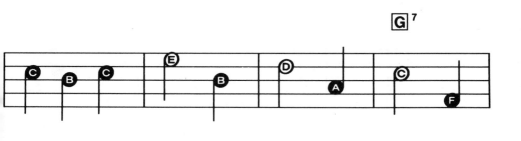

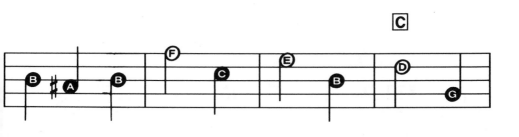

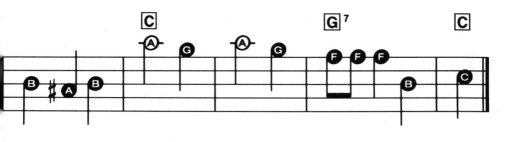

THE YELLOW ROSE OF TEXAS

Regi-Sound Program: 4
Rhythm: March or Fox Trot

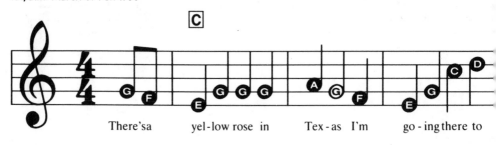

There'sa yel-low rose in Tex-as I'm go-ingthere to

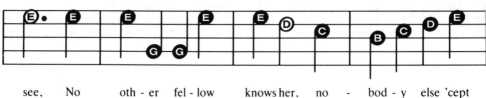

see, No oth-er fel-low knows her, no - bod-y else 'cept

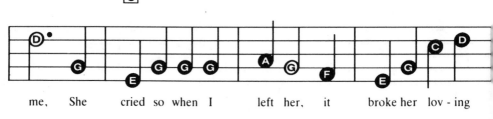

me, She cried so when I left her, it broke her lov-ing

heart and if we ev - er meet a - gain we'll

nev - er, nev - er, part. She's the sweet - est rose of

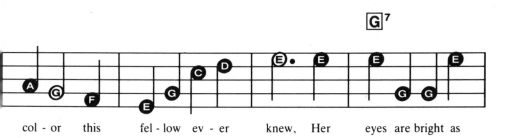

col - or this fel - low ev - er knew, Her eyes are bright as

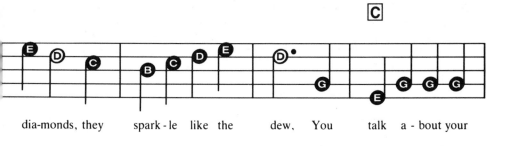

dia - monds, they spark - le like the dew, You talk a - bout your

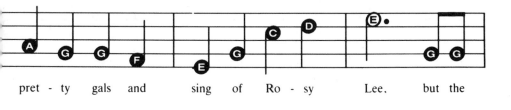

pret - ty gals and sing of Ro - sy Lee, but the

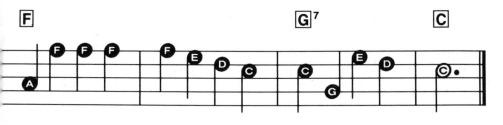

yel - low rose of Tex - as beats the belles of Ten - nes - see.

YOU TELL ME YOUR DREAM

Regi-Sound Program: 9
Rhythm: Waltz

You   had   a   dream,   Well,

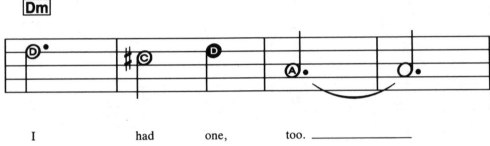

I   had   one,   too. ____

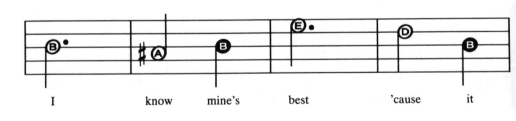

I   know   mine's   best   'cause   it

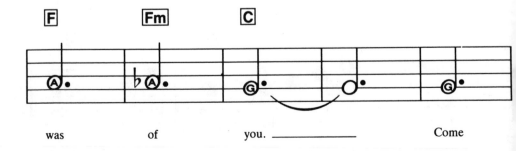

was   of   you. ____   Come

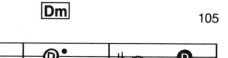

sweet - heart, tell   me,   Now   is   the

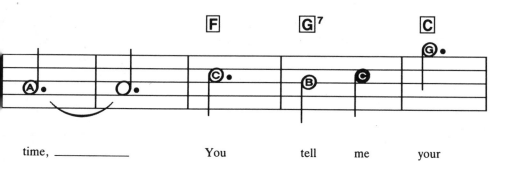

time, _____   You   tell   me   your

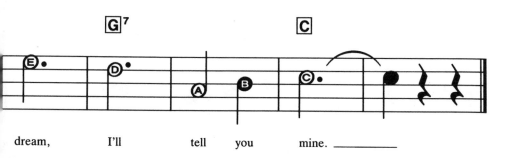

dream,   I'll   tell   you   mine. _____

HAVAH NAGILAH

Regi-Sound Program: 9
Rhythm: March or Polka

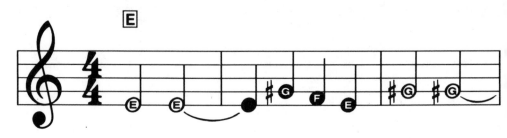

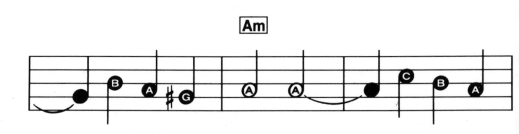

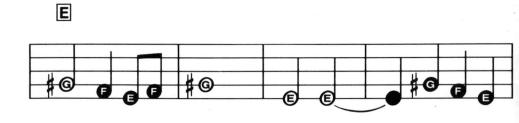

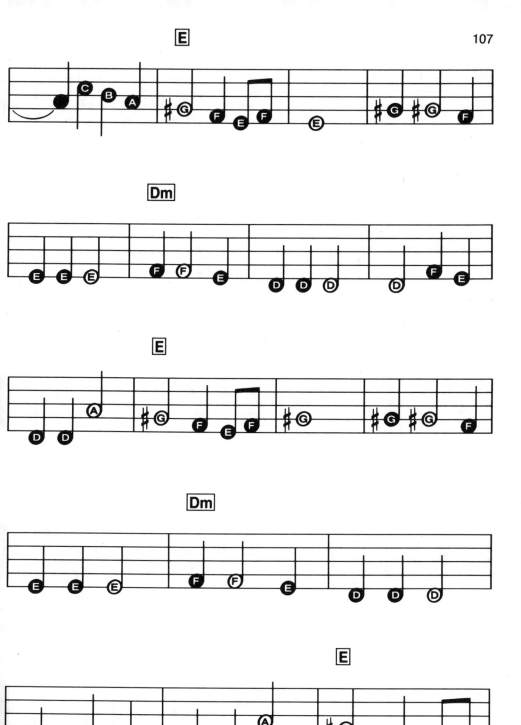

108

ALOUETTE

Regi-Sound Program: 9
Rhythm: Swing

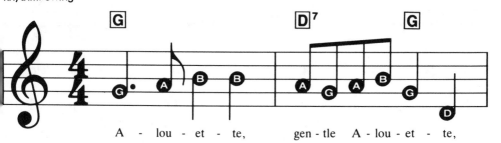

A - lou - et - te,   gen - tle A - lou - et - te,

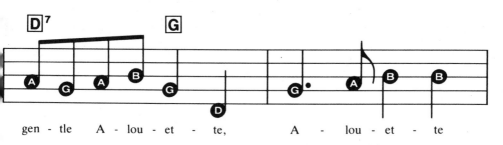

A - lou - et - te,   je te plu - me - rai.   A - lou - et - te,

gen - tle A - lou - et - te,   A - lou - et - te

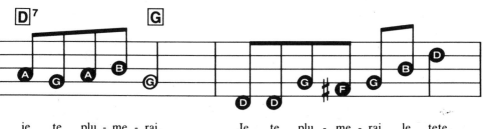

je te plu - me - rai.   Je te plu - me - rai le tete,

je te plu - me - rai la tete. Et la tete et la tete,

Oh! A - lou - et - te, gen - tle A - lou - et - te,

A - lou - et - te, je te plu - me - rai.

ARE YOU SLEEPING

Regi-Sound Program: 9
Rhythm: Swing

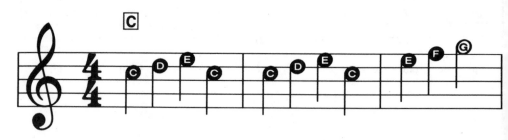

Are you sleep-ing? Are you sleep-ing? Broth-er John,

Broth-er John.   Morn-ing bells are ring-ing,   morn-ing bells are ring-ing,

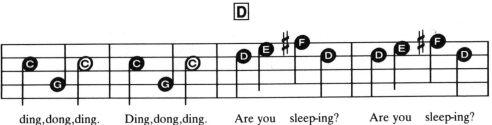

D

ding,dong,ding.   Ding,dong,ding.   Are you sleep-ing?   Are you sleep-ing?

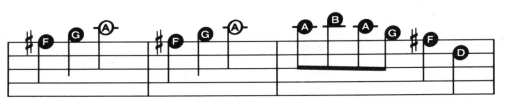

Broth - er John,   Broth - er John.   Morn - ing bells are   ring - ing,

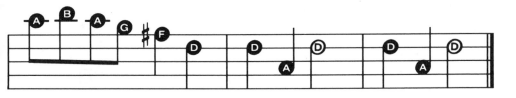

morn - ing bells are   ring - ing,   ding, dong, ding.   Ding, dong, ding.

A BIRD IN A GILDED CAGE

Regi-Sound Program: 8
Rhythm: Waltz

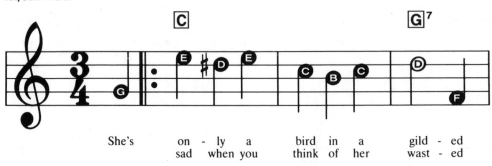

She's on - ly a bird in a gild - ed
sad when you think of her wast - ed

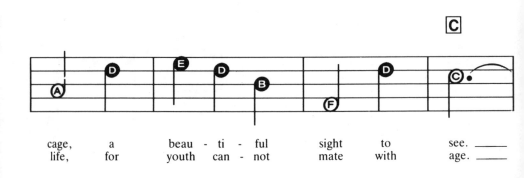

cage, a beau - ti - ful sight to see. _____
life, for youth can - not mate with age. _____

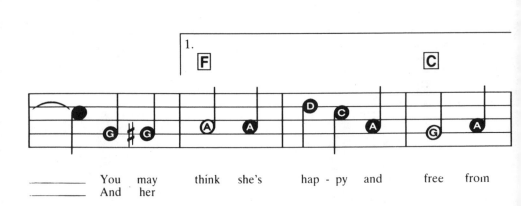

1.

_____ You may think she's hap - py and free from
_____ And her

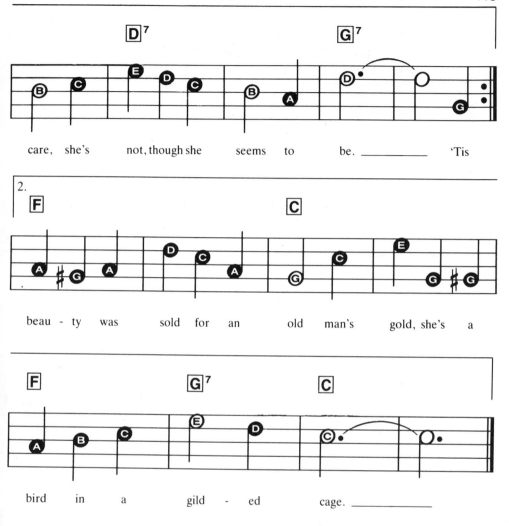

D⁷			G⁷		

care, she's not, though she seems to be. _____ 'Tis

beau - ty was sold for an old man's gold, she's a

bird in a gild - ed cage. _____

BIRTHDAY SONG

Regi-Sound Program: 8
Rhythm: Waltz

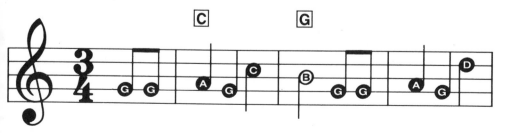

WEDDING MARCH
(BRIDAL CHORUS)

Regi-Sound Program: 6
Rhythm: March

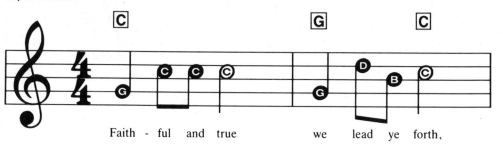

Faith - ful and true   we lead ye forth,

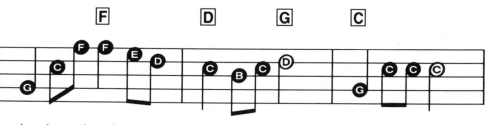

where love tri-umph-ant shall   crown ye with joy!   Star of re-nown,

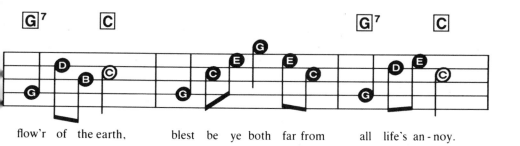

flow'r of the earth,   blest be ye both far from   all life's an - noy.

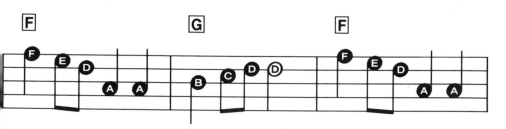

Cham-pion vic - tor - ious,   go thou be - fore!   Maid bright and glo - rious,

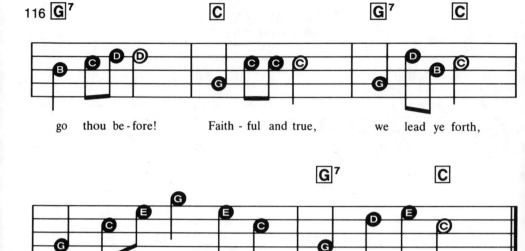

go thou be - fore! Faith - ful and true, we lead ye forth,

where love tri - umph - ant shall crown ye with joy!

BY THE LIGHT OF THE SILVERY MOON

Regi-Sound Program: 8
Rhythm: Swing

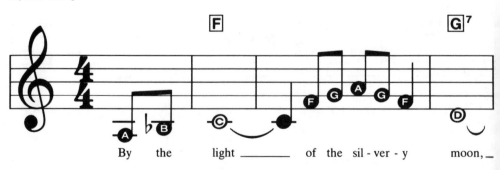

By the light _____ of the sil - ver - y moon, _

I want to spoon, _____ To my hon-ey I'll croon love's

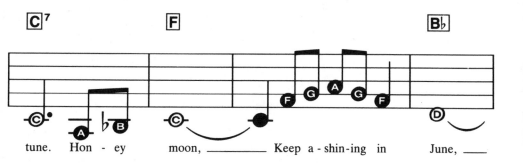

tune. Hon - ey moon, _____ Keep a-shin-ing in June, ____

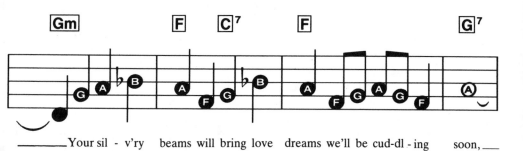

_____ Your sil - v'ry beams will bring love dreams we'll be cud-dl-ing soon, ___

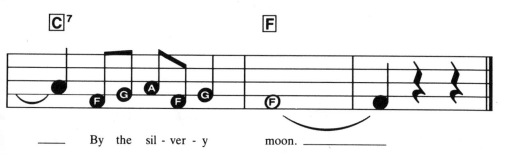

_____ By the sil - ver - y moon. _____

CARNIVAL OF VENICE

Regi-Sound Program: 5
Rhythm: Waltz

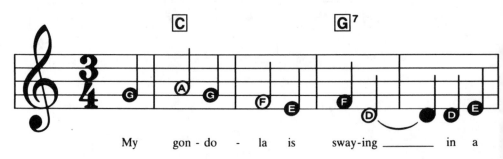

My gon-do-la is sway-ing _____ in a

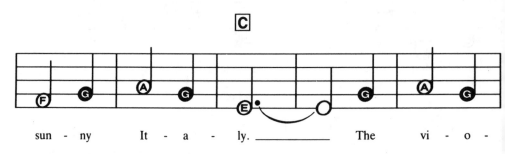

sun - ny It - a - ly. _____ The vi - o -

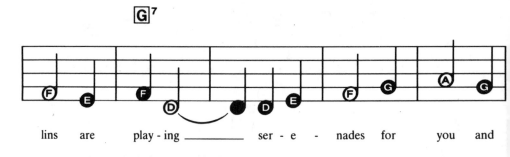

lins are play-ing _____ ser - e - nades for you and

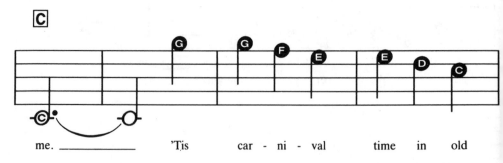

me. _____ 'Tis car - ni - val time in old

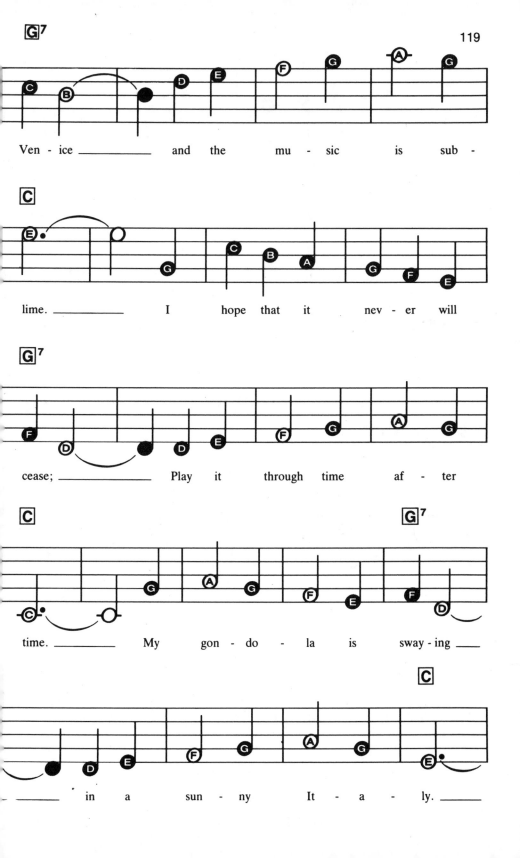

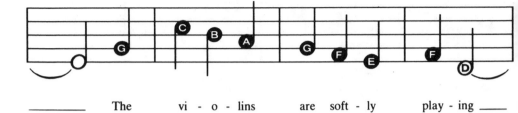

The vi - o - lins are soft - ly play - ing _____

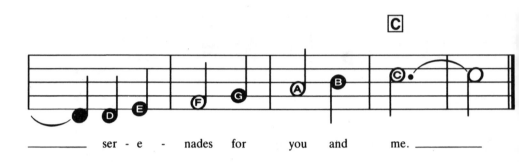

_____ ser - e - nades for you and me. _____

CIRIBIRIBIN

Regi-Sound Program: 4
Rhythm: Waltz

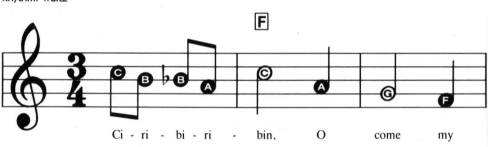

Ci - ri - bi - ri - bin, O come my

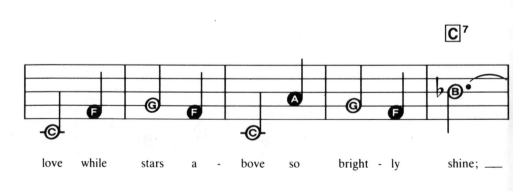

love while stars a - bove so bright - ly shine;

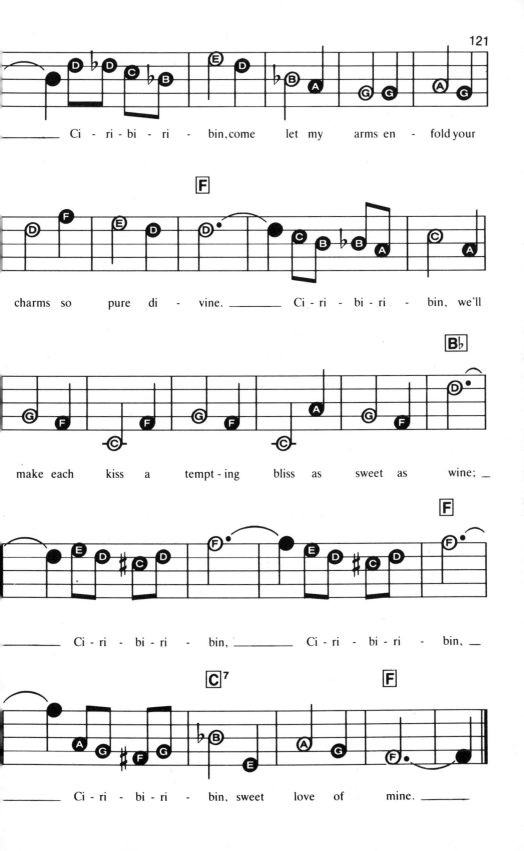

COCKLES AND MUSSELS

Regi-Sound Program: 9
Rhythm: Waltz

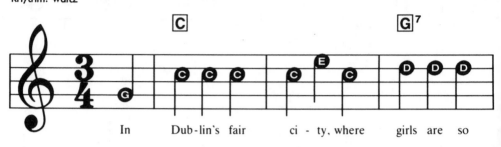

In Dub-lin's fair ci - ty, where girls are so

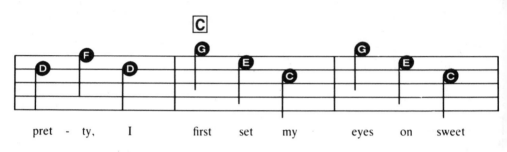

pret - ty, I first set my eyes on sweet

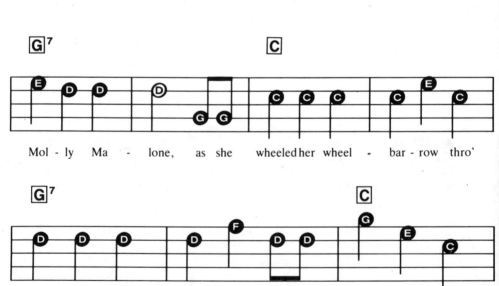

Mol - ly Ma - lone, as she wheeled her wheel - bar - row thro'

streets broad and nar - row, cry - ing "Cock - les and

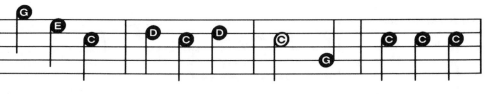

Mus - sels A - live, A - live, O!" A - live, A - live,

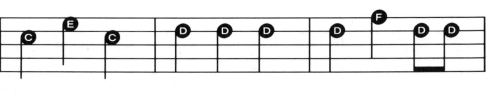

O! _____ A - live A - live O! _____ cry - ing

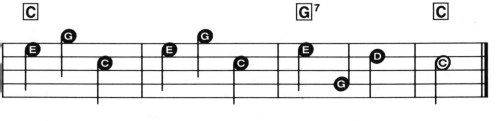

"Cock - les and Mus - sels A - live, A - live, O!"

CUDDLE UP A LITTLE CLOSER, LOVEY MINE

Regi-Sound Program: 1
Rhythm: Swing

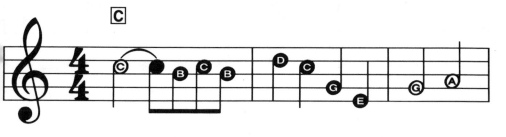

Cud - dle up a lit - tle clos - er, lov - ey

124 **G**⁷

mine,   Cud - dle up and be my lit - tle

C   **A**⁷

cling - ing   vine.   Like to feel your cheek so

D⁷   **G**⁷   **Am**

ro - sy,   Like to make you com - fy,   co - zy

D⁷   **C**   **D**⁷ **G**⁷   **C**

'Cause I love from head to   toe - sy,   lov - ey   mine. __

EL CHOCLO

Regi-Sound Program: 9
Rhythm: Latin or Beguine

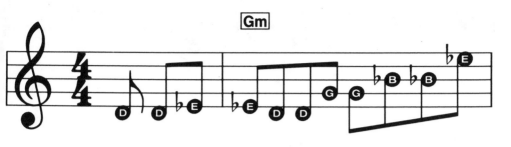

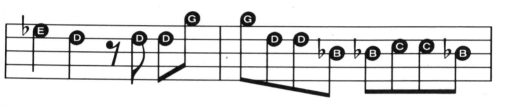

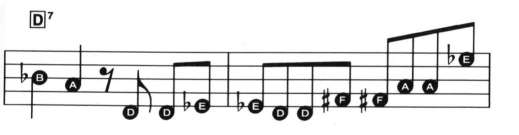

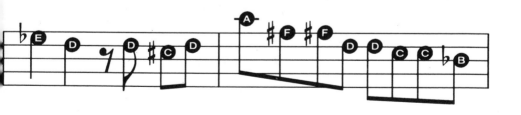

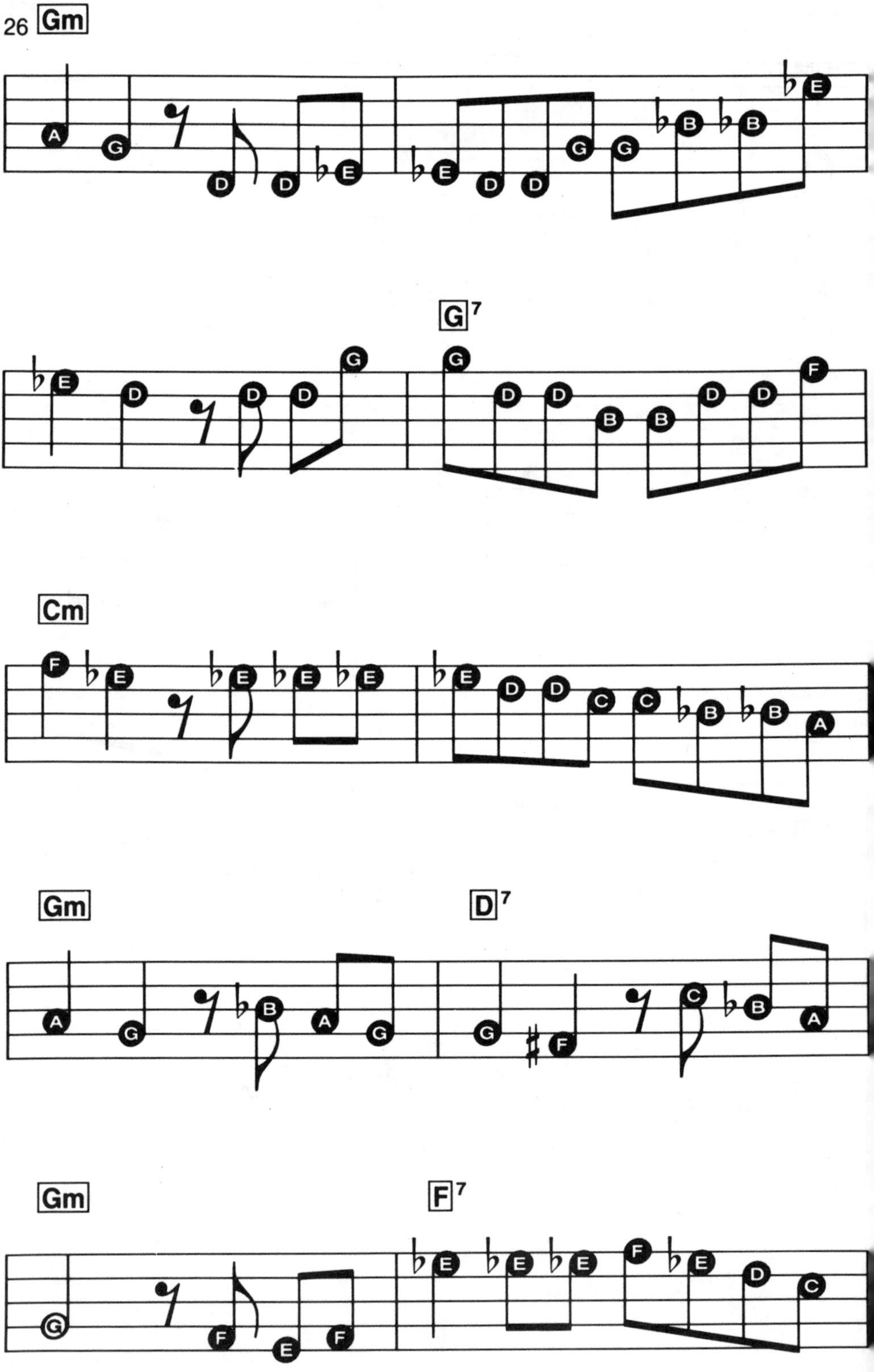
Gm
G7
Cm
Gm
D7
Gm
F7

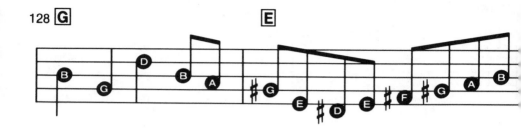

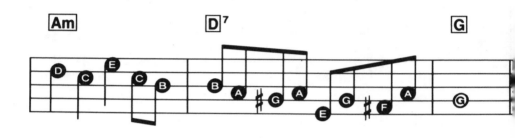

THE ENTERTAINER

Regi-Sound Program: 8
Rhythm: Swing

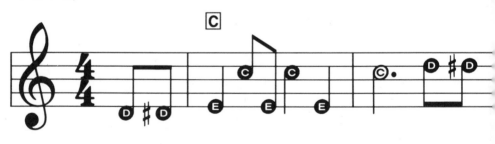

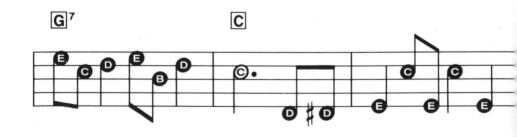

FOR HE'S A JOLLY GOOD FELLOW

und Program: 4
Waltz

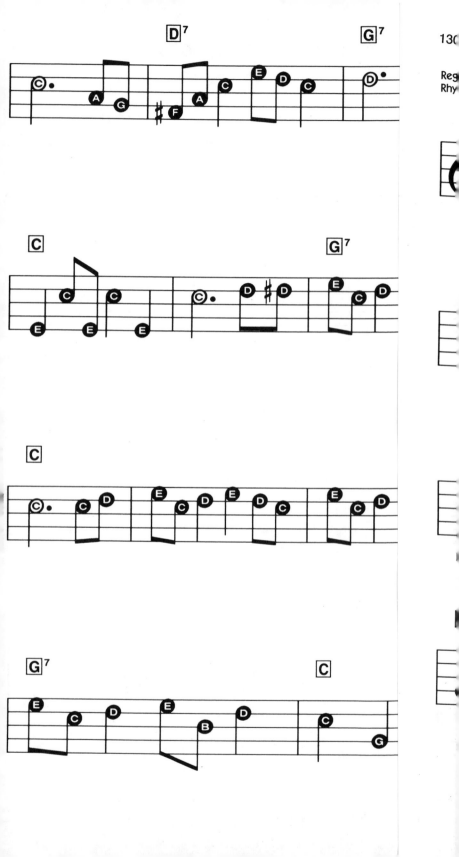

Reg
Rhy

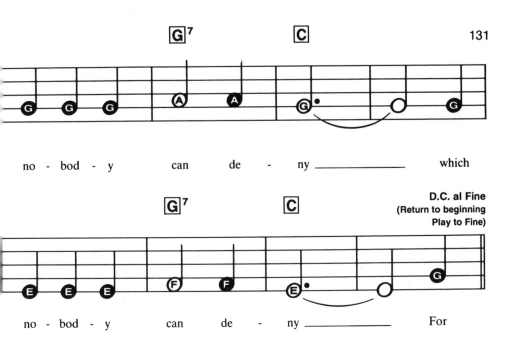

no - bod - y can de - ny _____ which

no - bod - y can de - ny _____ For

HELLO! MY BABY

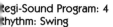

Regi-Sound Program: 4
Rhythm: Swing

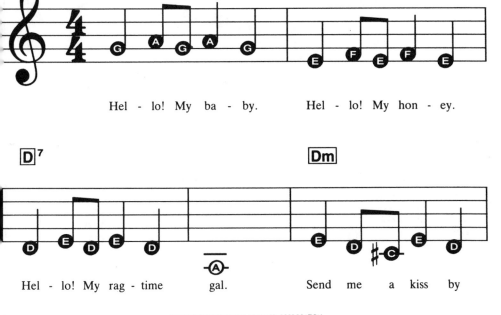

Hel - lo! My ba - by.   Hel - lo! My hon - ey.

Hel - lo! My rag - time   gal.   Send me a kiss by

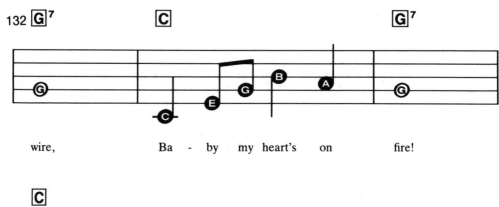

wire,   Ba - by   my   heart's   on   fire!

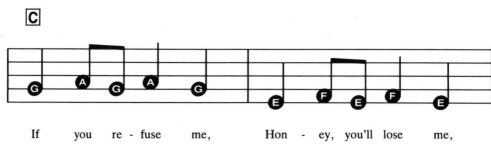

If   you   re - fuse   me,   Hon - ey, you'll lose   me,

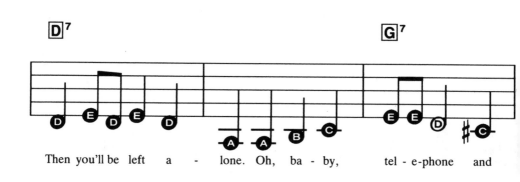

Then you'll be left   a   -   lone. Oh, ba - by,   tel - e-phone and

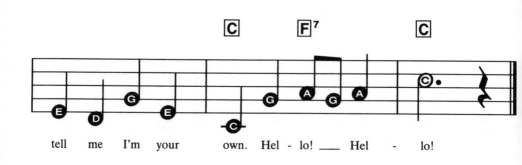

tell   me   I'm   your   own. Hel - lo! __ Hel - lo!

GRANDFATHER'S CLOCK

Regi-Sound Program: 4
Rhythm: Swing

al - ways his treas - ure and pride. _____ But it

stopped! Short! Nev - er to go a -

gain, when the old man died! _____

HUMORESQUE

Regi-Sound Program: 9
Rhythm: Swing

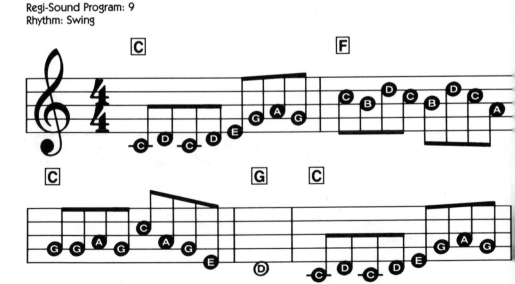

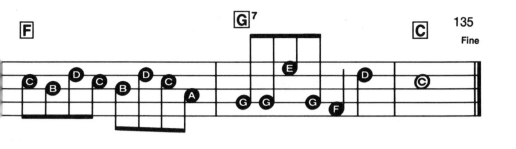

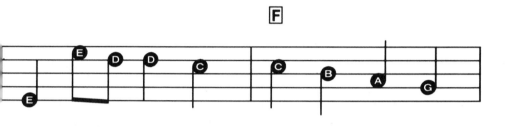

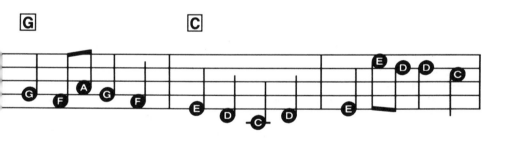

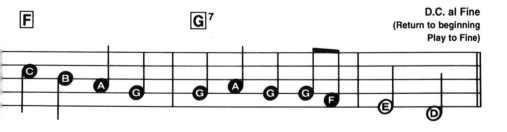

GREENSLEEVES

Regi-Sound Program: 3
Rhythm: Waltz

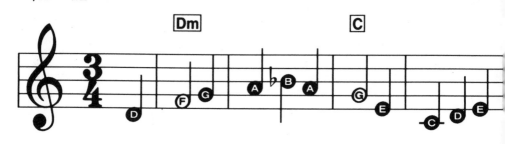

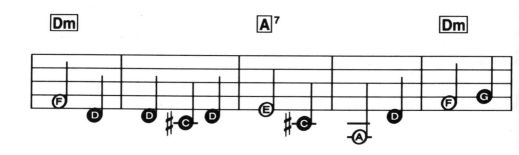

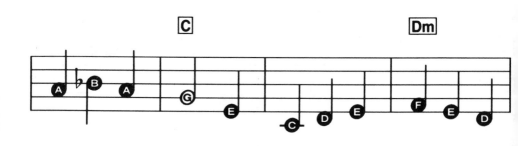

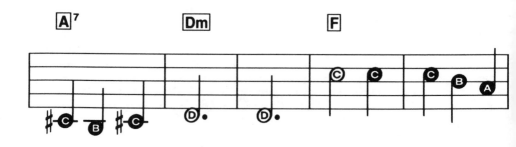

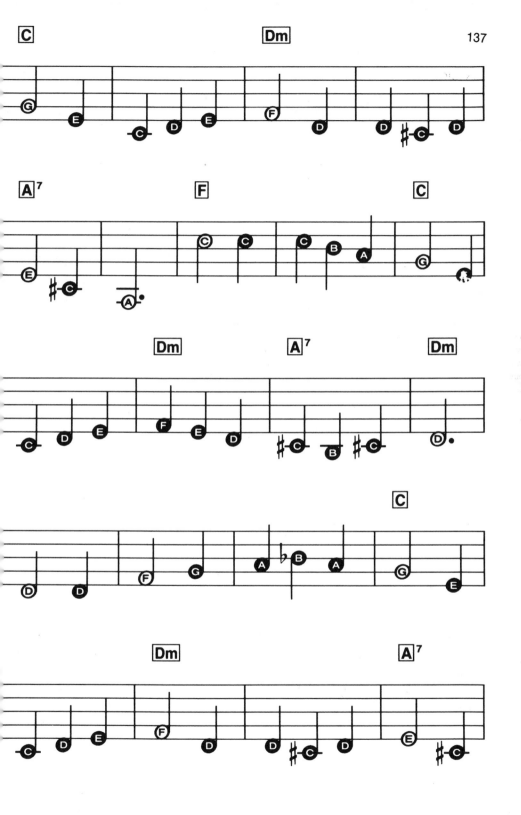

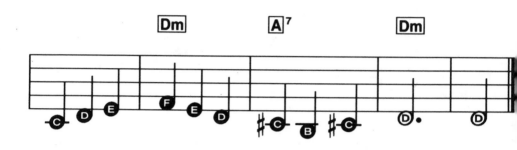

IN MY MERRY OLDSMOBILE

Regi-Sound Program: 4
Rhythm: Waltz

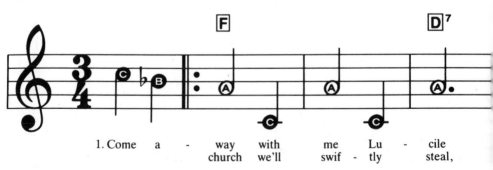

1. Come a - way with me Lu - cile
church we'll swif - tly steal,

LA GOLONDRINA

Regi-Sound Program: 9
Rhythm: Waltz

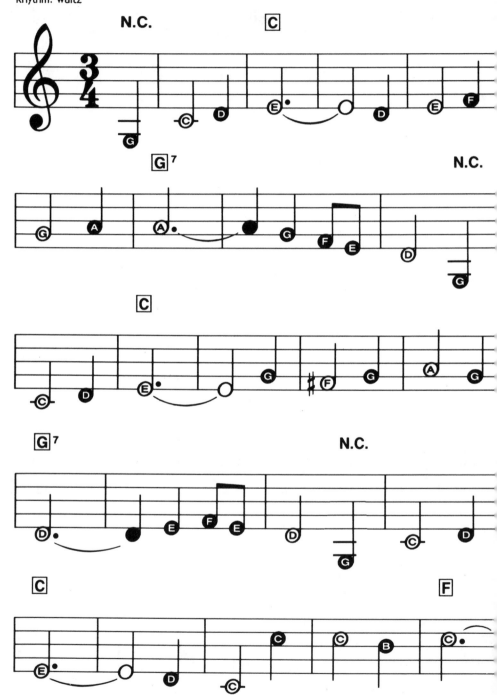

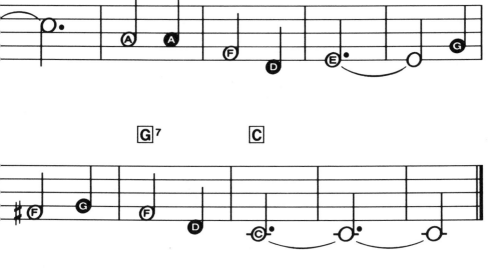

LONG, LONG AGO

Regi-Sound Program: 10
Rhythm: Swing

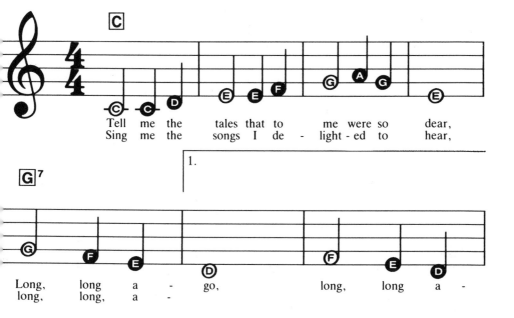

Tell me the tales that to me were so dear,
Sing me the songs I de - light - ed to hear,

Long, long a - go, long, long a -
long, long, a -

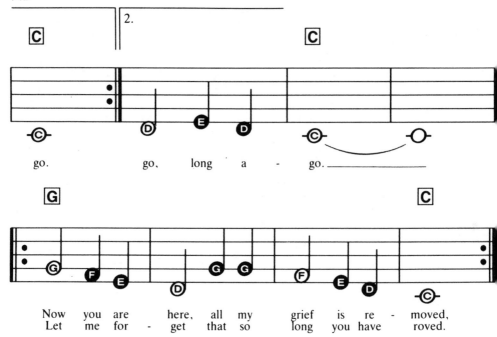

go.   go, long a - go. _____

Now you are   here, all my   grief is re - moved,
Let   me for - get that so   long you have   roved.

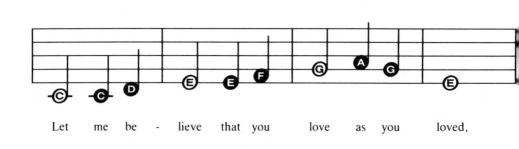

Let me be - lieve that you   love   as you   loved,

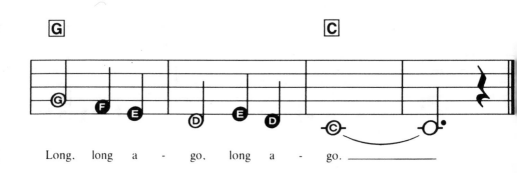

Long, long a - go, long a - go. _____

LONDON BRIDGE

Regi-Sound Program: 9
Rhythm: Swing

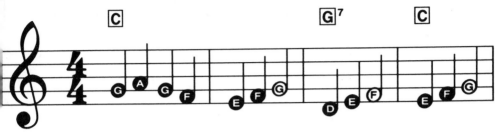

Lon-don bridge is   fall-ingdown,   fall-ingdown   fall-ingdown,

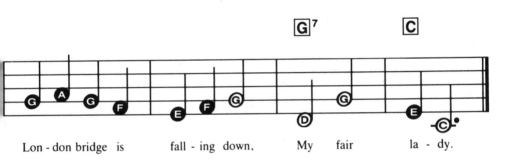

Lon - don bridge is   fall - ing down,   My   fair   la - dy.

MARY'S A GRAND OLD NAME

Regi-Sound Program: 9
Rhythm: Swing

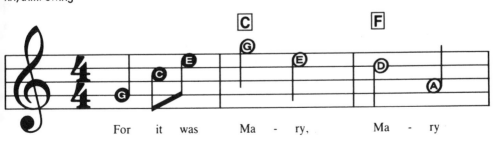

For   it was   Ma - ry,   Ma - ry

MELODY OF LOVE

Regi-Sound Program: 9
Rhythm: Waltz

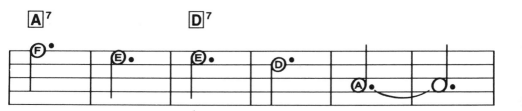

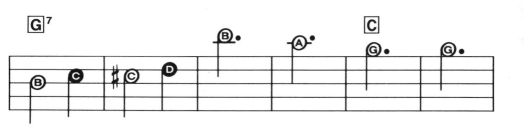

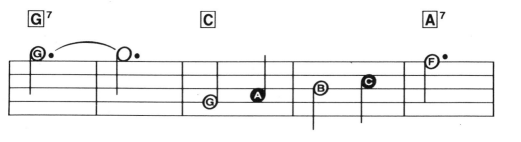

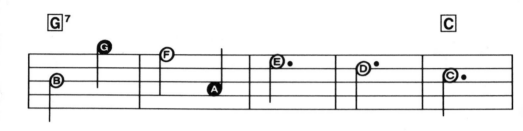

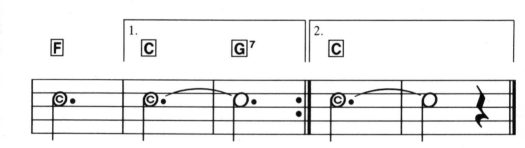

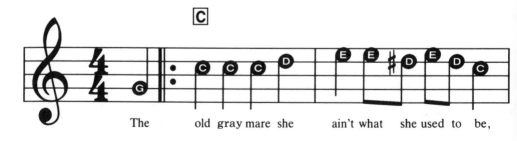

THE OLD GRAY MARE

Regi-Sound Program: 4
Rhythm: Swing

The old gray mare she ain't what she used to be,

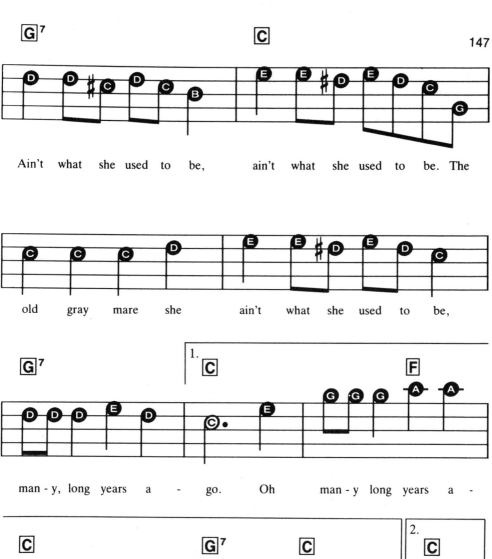

Ain't what she used to be, ain't what she used to be. The

old gray mare she ain't what she used to be,

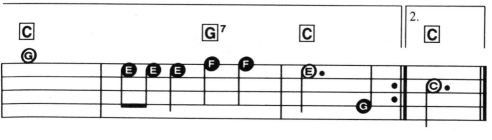

man - y, long years a - go. Oh man - y long years a -

go, man - y long years a - go The go.

MINUET

Regi-Sound Program: 6
Rhythm: Waltz

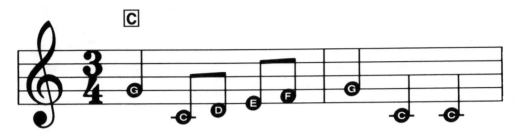

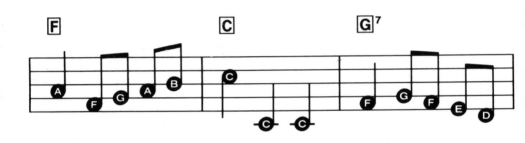

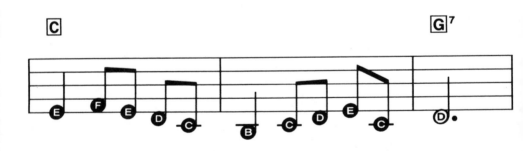

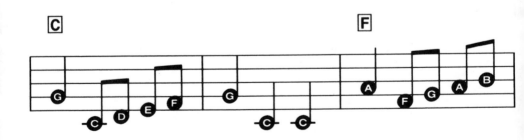

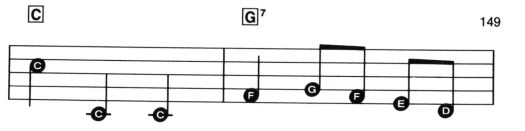

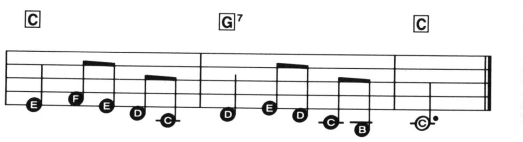

OLD MacDONALD

Regi-Sound Program: 9
Rhythm: Swing

1. Old Mac-Don-ald had a farm, Ee - igh, ee - igh,

oh! And   on that farm he   had some (chicks),   Ee - igh, ee - igh,

oh!   with   a   (chick, chick) here   and   a   (chick, chick) there,

here   a (chick), there   a (chick),   ev - 'ry - where   a   (chick, chick)*

Old Mac-Don-ald   had   a   farm,   Ee - igh, ee - igh,   oh!

2. ducks - quack, quack
3. turkeys - gobble, gobble
4. pigs - oink, oink
5. cows - moo, moo
6. donkeys - hee haw
7. sheep - baa, baa

*Each time you add a new animal, keep repeating the measures between
① and ② and sing about them backward until you get back to the first
animal (chicks - chick, chick). Then, continue to the end of the song.

ON TOP OF OLD SMOKEY

Regi-Sound Program: 4
Rhythm: Waltz

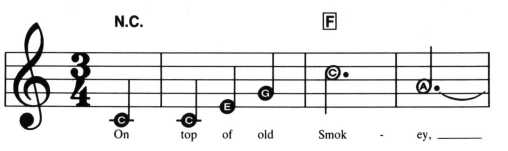

On   top   of   old   Smok - ey, _____

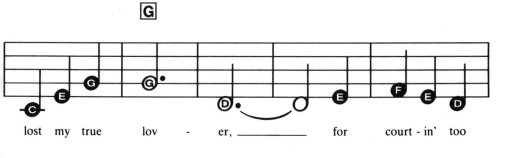

_____   all   cov - ered   with   snow, _____   I

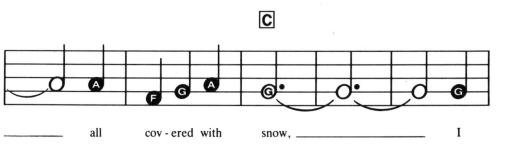

lost   my   true   lov - er, _____   for   court - in'   too

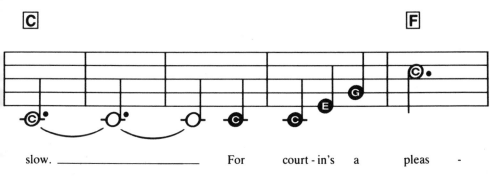

slow. _____   For   court - in's   a   pleas -

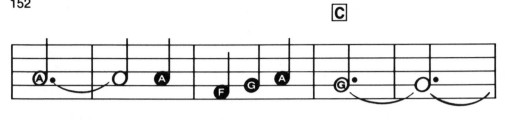

ure, _____ and flirt - in' is grief; _____

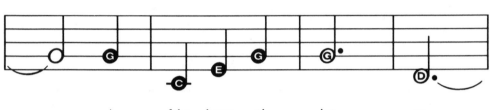

_____ A false - heart - ed lov - er, _____

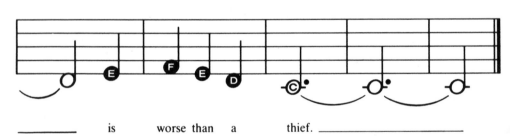

_____ is worse than a thief. _____

OUR DIRECTOR

Regi-Sound Program: 4
Rhythm: March or Polka

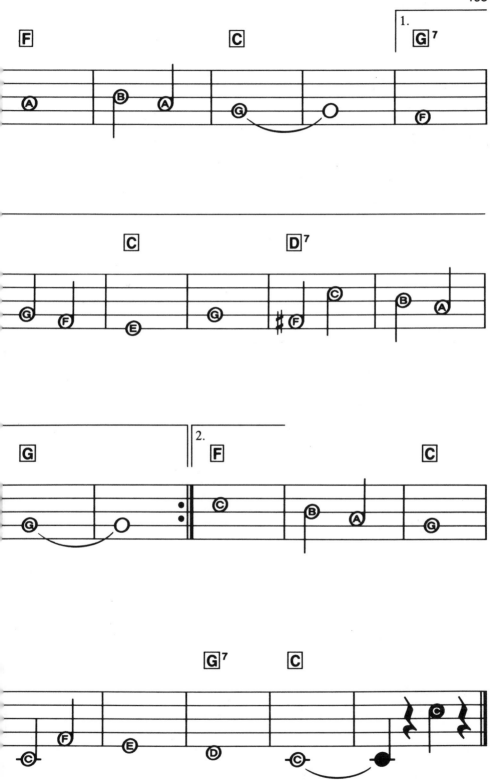

PUT ON YOUR OLD GRAY BONNET

Regi-Sound Program: 7
Rhythm: Swing

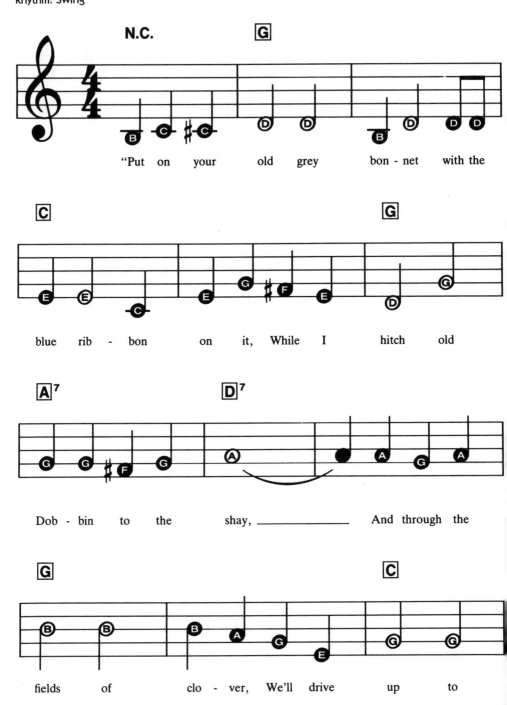

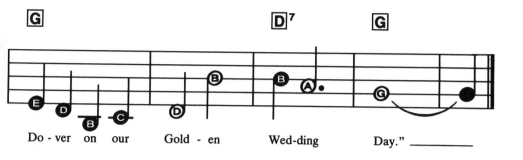

Do - ver on our Gold - en Wed - ding Day." _____

SHINE ON, HARVEST MOON

Regi-Sound Program: 7
Rhythm: Swing

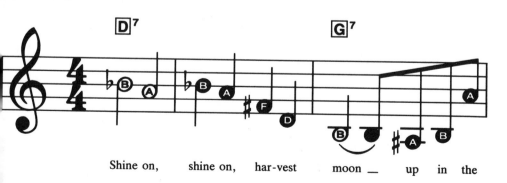

Shine on, shine on, har-vest moon __ up in the

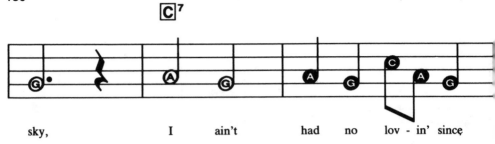

sky,   I   ain't   had   no   lov - in' since

Jan - u - ar - y, Feb - ru - a - ry,   June or Ju - ly.

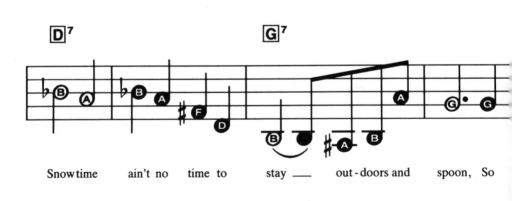

Snow time ain't no time to   stay — out - doors and spoon, So

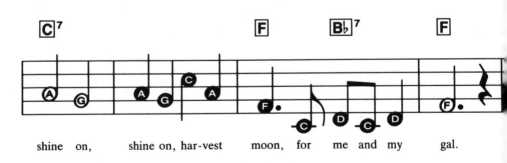

shine on,   shine on, har - vest moon, for me and my   gal.

BARCAROLLE

egi-Sound Program: 1
hythm: Waltz

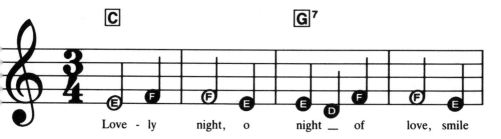

Love - ly night, o night _ of love, smile

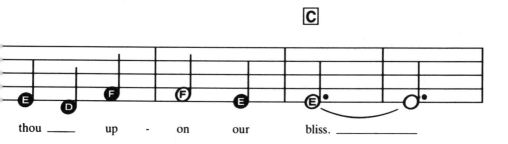

thou _ up - on our bliss. _____

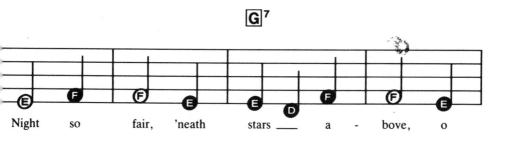

Night so fair, 'neath stars _ a - bove, o

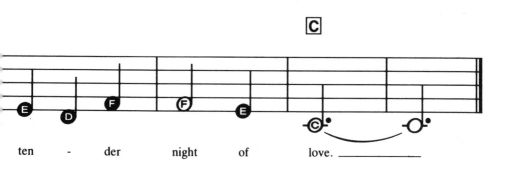

ten - der night of love. _____

THE BLUE TAIL FLY
(a/k/a JIMMY CRACK CORN)

Regi-Sound Program: 9
Rhythm: Swing

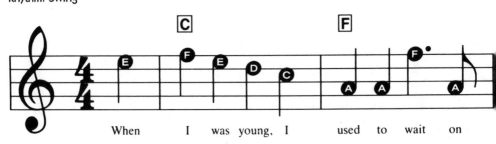

When I was young, I used to wait on

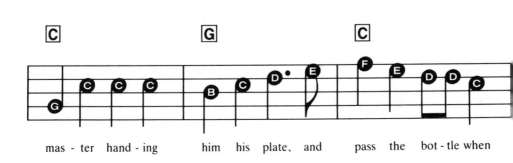

mas - ter hand - ing him his plate, and pass the bot - tle when

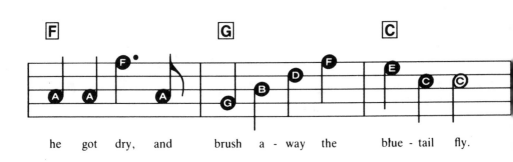

he got dry, and brush a - way the blue - tail fly.

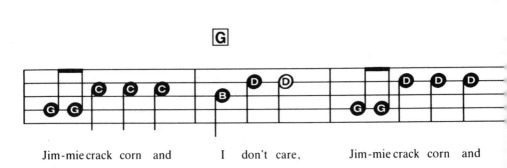

Jim - mie crack corn and I don't care, Jim - mie crack corn and

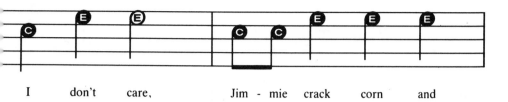

I don't care, Jim - mie crack corn and

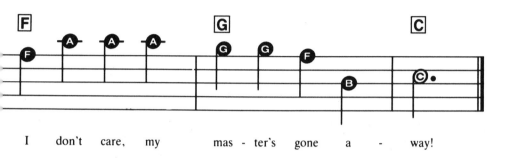

I don't care, my mas - ter's gone a - way!

SONG OF INDIA

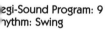
egi-Sound Program: 9
hythm: Swing

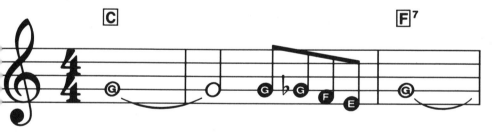

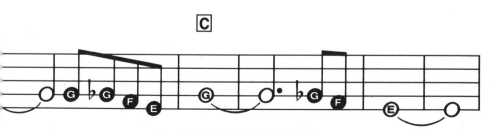

SING A SONG OF SIXPENCE

egi-Sound Program: 4
hythm: Swing

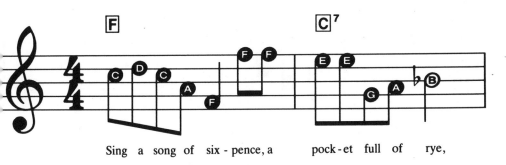

Sing a song of six - pence, a   pock - et full of   rye,

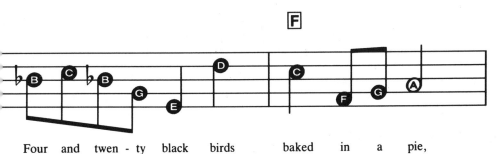

Four and twen - ty black birds   baked   in   a   pie,

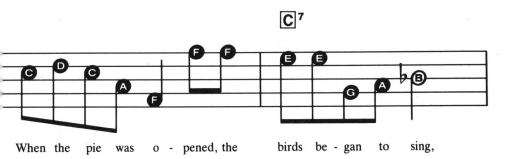

When the pie was o - pened, the   birds be - gan to   sing,

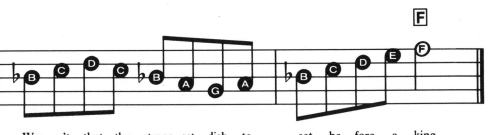

Was - n't that the strang - est dish to   set be - fore a king.

BLUE DANUBE WALTZ

Regi-Sound Program: 9
Rhythm: Waltz

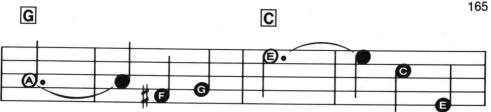

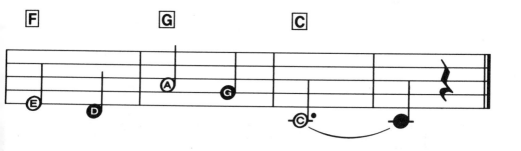

THE GLOW WORM

Regi-Sound Program: 8
Rhythm: Swing

Shine, lit - tle glow - worm, glim - mer, (glim - mer,)

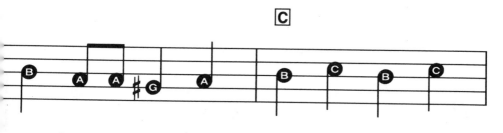

Shine, lit - tle glow - worm, glim - mer! (glim - mer!)

166

Lead us, lest too far we wan - der, Love's sweet voice is

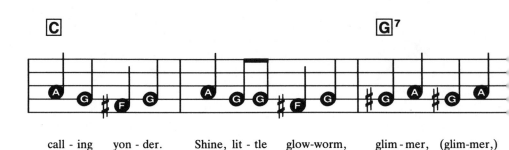

call - ing yon - der. Shine, lit - tle glow-worm, glim - mer, (glim-mer,)

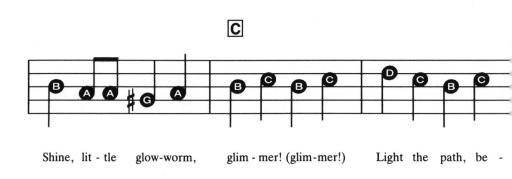

Shine, lit - tle glow-worm, glim - mer! (glim-mer!) Light the path, be -

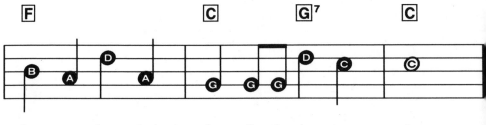

low, a - bove, And glow, lit - tle glow - worm, glow.

THERE IS A TAVERN IN THE TOWN

Regi-Sound Program: 4
Rhythm: March or Fox Trot

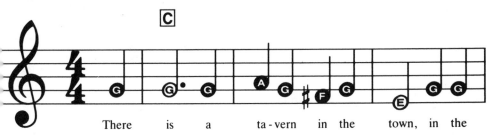

There is a ta-vern in the town, in the

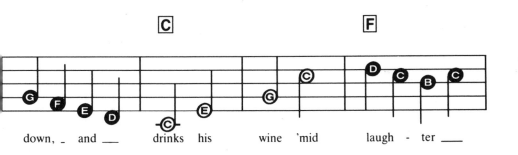

town, And where my true love sits him down, sits him

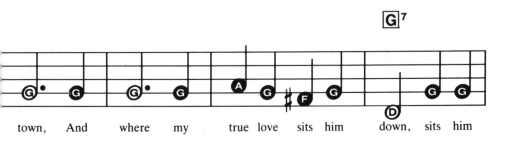

down, _ and __ drinks his wine 'mid laugh - ter ____

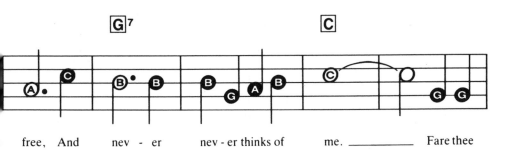

free, And nev - er nev - er thinks of me. ____ Fare thee

168

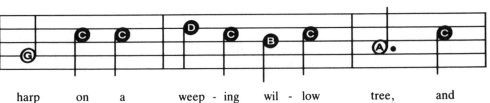

harp   on   a   weep - ing   wil - low   tree,   and

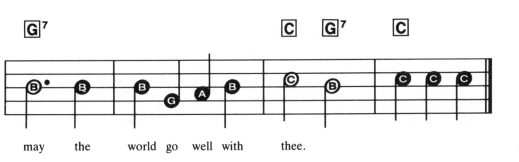

may   the   world   go   well   with   thee.

WILLIAM TELL OVERTURE

Regi-Sound Program: 4
Rhythm: March or Polka

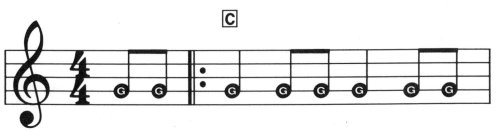

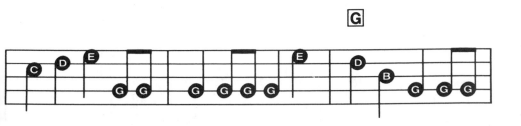

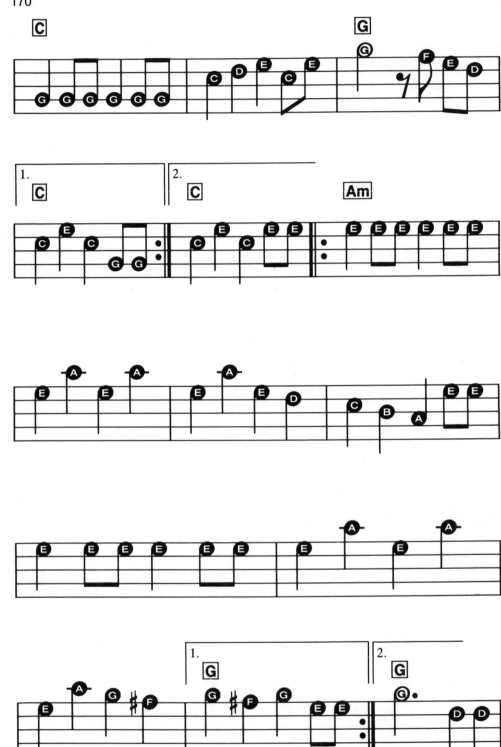

171

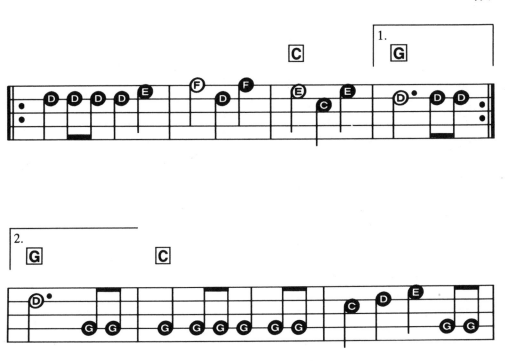

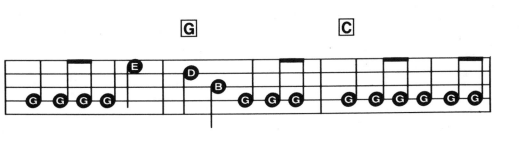

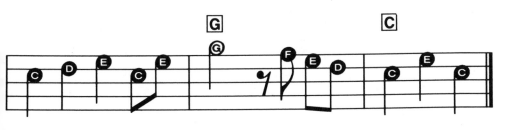

TOM DOOLEY

Regi-Sound Program: 9
Rhythm: Swing

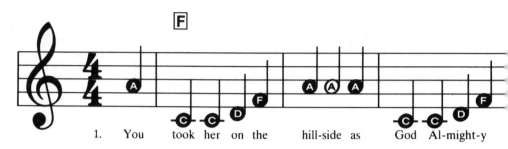

1. You took her on the hill-side as God Al-might-y

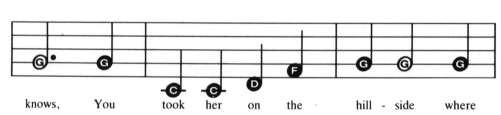

knows, You took her on the hill - side where

Chorus

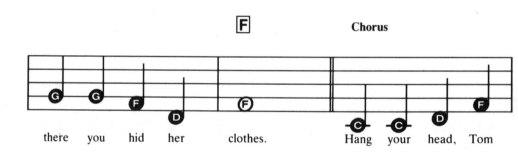

there you hid her clothes. Hang your head, Tom

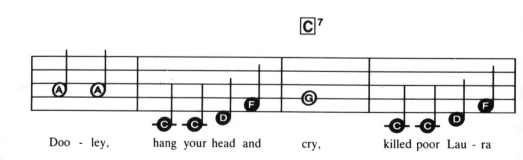

Doo - ley, hang your head and cry, killed poor Lau - ra

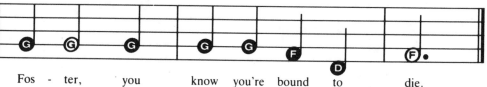

Fos - ter, you know you're bound to die.

2. You took her by the roadside where you begged to be excused,
You took her by the roadside where there you hid her shoes.
Chorus

3. You took her on the hillside to make her your wife,
You took her on the hillside where there you took her life.
Chorus

4. Take down my old violin and play it all you please,
At this time tomorrow it'll be no use to me.
Chorus

5. I dug a grave four feet long, I dug it three feet deep,
And throwed the cold clay o'er her head and tramped it with my feet.
Chorus

6. This world and one more, then where do you reckon I'd be.
If it hadn't been for Grayson I'd-a-been in Tennessee.
Chorus

YANKEE DOODLE

Regi-Sound Program: 4
Rhythm: March or Polka

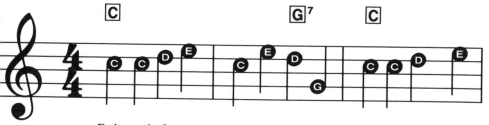

Father and I went down to camp a - long with Cap - tain
There we saw a thou-sand men, as rich as Squire ___

174

Good - ing And   there we saw the   men and boys as
Da - vid And   what they wast - ed   ev - 'ry day I

thick as ha - sty   pud - ding.   Yan - kee Doo - dle   keep it up,
wish it could be   sav - ed.

Yan - kee Doo - dle   dan - dy,   Mind the mu - sic

and the step, And   with the girls be   hand - y.   hand - y.